240

Wallace Brown

This ble. puts the case well —
is consistent in argument / Scap —
but is terribly conservative.

AN ORIGINAL WORK

THE
DIVORCE PROBLEM

Being

A Biblical Treatise on the subject of
divorce in relation to: Marriage as constituted in the beginning; the Law of
Moses; the Kingdom of God; Church
doctrine; Church order; and Christian
practice.

THE
DIVORCE PROBLEM

FULLY DISCUSSED
AND
A SCRIPTURAL SOLUTION

FIRST EDITION
1952
MacNeish Publishers
6 S. Church St., Waynesboro, Pa., U.S.A.

INSCRIPTION

With affection and esteem I inscribe
this treatise to Mr. and Mrs. Alexander
Wilson and family, of McKeesport, Pa.,
U. S. A.

TABLE OF CONTENTS

CONCLUSION

FOREWORD

By Professor *H. L. Ellison*, B.A., B.D., London, England

I am no friend of the practice of writing commendatory forewords for I believe that a good book is its best commendation, but for Mr. Fisher-Hunter I have gladly made an exception. This is not due to personal friendship, for we have never met, but to the importance of his theme and the essential soundness of his treatment of it.

Naturally this does not imply that I should have expressed everything as he has. In particular I am convinced that his treatment of Deut. 24:1-4 is based on a misunderstanding of its meaning. But his general conclusions I can accept without reservation.

Before a Christian or a church tolerates divorce proceedings by a Christian it is not enough to quote Matth. 5:32 or 19:9. The following questions must be faced and answered. Why did the early Church forbid *every* form of divorce? It was not until Christianity became the official religion of the Roman empire and the heathen flooded unconverted into the Church that divorce was permitted. In the West the Church of Rome, in spite of its growing errors, could not bring itself to agree that the New Testament permitted divorce and so invented a back-door instead.

If Christian marriage is a picture of the love of Christ to the Church (Eph. 5:22-33), does not permission to break a marriage by divorce imply of necessity that there are sins that Jesus Christ cannot forgive in a Christian and that will lead to his eternal rejection, for the Bible excludes the possibility that a couple that have divorced should later re-marry one another,

1

but we're not X's — an ideal, but not possible?

If our Lord had not intended to forbid divorce, why did the Holy Spirit allow Mark and Luke to lead so many early Christians astray? It was not until well on in the second century that every church will have had all four gospels.

If our Lord was in fact allowing divorce in a strictly limited number of cases, viz. where adultery had taken place, why did He use deliberately misleading language, for nowhere else in the New Testament does fornication mean adultery? The attempts to prove the contrary are so weak that it is difficult to believe in many cases that they are not merely sops to a guilty conscience or excuses for slack church discipline. The force of this question cannot be evaded by the counter-question, what then does fornication mean? Whether Mr. Fisher-Hunter is correct in his argument that in these two Matthew passages our Lord is addressing Himself to Jews and bringing home to them that they had gone beyond the limits of Deut. 24:1-4, or whether it means concealed pre-marital unchastity as envisaged in Deut. 22:13-21, or marriages forbidden in Lev. 18., as is perhaps suggested by Acts 15:20, 29, is immaterial. The uncertainty does not make the word mean adultery, nor does it offer any relief to the man who has promised life-long fidelity to his wife, or vice versa, and now wants to break his promise.

One of the worst of the passions that enslaved the Gentile world in the days of our Lord was the corruption of sex. The Christian's freedom from sexual bondage startled the heathen and convinced them of the power of the risen Lord. Except that sexual promiscuity is still not altogether respectable, for millions in the Anglo-Saxon lands conditions are very like those of the first century A.D. In

2

1939 the Registrar-General's figures show that one in six of first babies born that year in England (ignoring illegitimate children) had been conceived before its mother's marriage. When we remember that babies are not always the wages of sexual sin and also the increasing knowledge of contraceptives, we will not be far out in saying that even before the war in England one bride in three was no longer a virgin. In the United States it is obvious that marriage for millions is only a legalizing of promiscuity, for they take it for granted that they can divorce whenever they want to marry someone else.

The excuse for this attitude of mind and behaviour is that sex is natural. The Gospel will not be respected unless the Church shows the world that the power of Christ is supernatural, able to control all that is natural. Let us not deceive ourselves. Apart from a limited number of really hard cases—and is not the grace of Christ sufficient there?—the real motive behind most divorce cases in which Christians are involved is the desire to be free to marry again. For the worldling such cases are only the sure evidence that the Christian is as sex-enthralled as the rest.

May this book be widely read and awaken many Christians to the implications of Christ's lordship in matters of sex.

Introduction

I am well aware of the fact that the subject on which I write is a thorny issue. It is also said to be a highly controversial theme which should be left unmentioned in ministry because of the offense and strife it might produce. I admit it to be controversial, but cannot the same thing be said of many Scriptural Subjects. *As Divorce is a matter of Christian conduct* it ought to be free from *controversy*, and I am sure that a close study of scripture will here, as in all matters of walk, answer the question beyond controversy.

Often truth is withheld, hersey is not exposed, and error neither opposed nor corrected because of the fear of man, or on account of a desire to avoid contention and keep up the appearance of unity under the guise of liberality and love. Scripture and experience prove such acting as this to be one of the chief causes of decline in godliness and departure from the faith on the part of Israel and the Church.

"He that hath my word, let him speak my word faithfully' (Jer. 23:28). But in seeking to do this, I shall not allow my feelings of resentment towards the evil to lead me beyond the Word of God in maintaining righteousness. On the other hand, I shall guard against allowing human sympathy for the innocent sufferer to cause me to lower God's standard of righteousness, or set aside the demands of the Word of God.

The increase in divorces, together with the ignorance, misinformation, and the differences in opinions that exist among Christians on the subject of divorce and remarriage is my warrant for believing that such a book as this is needed.

There are three schools of thought in Christendom on the subject of divorce. (1) Those who believe a Christian has the right to divorce and remarry; (2) those who believe he has the right to divorce but not to remarry; (3) those who believe the Christian has no Scriptural right to divorce.

The surprising thing about these differences is that all three classes base their claim exclusively on the words of the Lord Jesus. This necessarily reflects on Christ for it connects his Name with the confusion.

One of the desires that entered into the cause of my writing on divorce sprang from the conviction that the Lord's words were being misappropriated by some one or more of these schools of opinion.

I had the conviction that if this were pointed out in print it would go a long way toward banishing the ignorance, removing the confusion and producing one uniform rule acceptable to the vast majority of Christians. In seeking to do this I have avoided technicality.

I write for all Christians for although all such are for various reasons divided into many corporate bodies, yet in the controversy over divorce they will be found standing together in two groups only. One of these believe the Christian has a right to divorce, while the other is adamant in its belief that when the Word of God is rightly divided and correctly interpreted and properly appropriated a Christian has no such privilege.

This treatise is an entirely independent work in the sense that it is not based on any work on divorce in print. Prior to writing I can only recall reading one article on the subject. This appeared in a monthly biblical Journal over thirty years ago. It was written to defend the practice of a Christian divorcing and remarrying on the ground of adultery. It seemed to me that one weakness in the evidence used by the writer in proving his case was, that he appealed to the writings of men rather than to the Scriptures. This deficiency was a deciding factor in causing me to produce a treatise based on the testimony of Scripture wherein the subject would be dealt with exhaustively from every viewpoint and angle.

My reason for connecting the two chapters (I and II) on marriage to the subject of divorce is that I am convinced that true marriage as constituted by God is basic to and the best evidence and witness for the belief that divorce is an unscriptural practice in the life of a Christian. I have written quite at length on the Mosaic statute of divorce (chapter 3). This was necessary from two points of view. First, in order to clearly establish beyond the shadow of a doubt what constituted the specific cause for divorce, ambiguously translated, ''some uncleanness'' Deut. 24:1). Secondly, I was convinced that a knowledge of the legalised cause for divorce under the law of Moses would be the best evidence in asertaining the proper interpretation of Matthew 5:32; 19:9 and in disproving that these verses teach divorce on the ground of adultery. Believing much of the differences in opinion on divorce hinges on the misappropriation of the Lord's words I have devoted three chapters (4, 5, 6), to them, wherein they are treated from a threefold point of view. Personal observations inclined me to believe that many Churches of the saints desired help on how to deal with divorced persons among them and with others who sought to join their fellowship. It was with sincere desire to help these Churches that I added the chapters dealing with fellowship, reception, and dis-

6

cipline. The closing chapters (12,13,14) deal with experience and are written and designed to show the two different practical consequences that are the result of obeying Scripture either perfectly or imperfectly apprehended.

SIXFOLD PURPOSE OF WRITING

The purpose of this treatise is sixfold. I would seek to prove by the Scriptures the following points: (1) that the marriage bond is absolutely indissoluble; (2) that adultery does not break the marriage tie; (3) that divorce as permitted by Moses was not designed to break up an established valid marriage; (4) that the privilege of divorce as stated in Matthew 5:32 and 19:9 belongs only to men under the law of Moses, and not to Christians; (5) that the term "fornication" as used by the Lord Jesus in connection with divorce does not mean adultery, but rather an illicit sexual act committed in the premarital state, or in a marital relation that is not a valid one; and (6) that the only Christian who has the right to remarry is the widow or the widower.

I trust what is written will be a light to prevent Christains from being involved in this evil, and a means in restraining any such who are divorced from entering into a permanent adulterous relationship through remarriage. Those who have a care for the Church (I Tim. 3:5) may find it helpful in their responsibility of sheperding God's flock and in maintaining order and holiness in God's house. Also, it is my fervent desire that the truths presented herein may be used in preventing any harsh and unjust treatment being meted out to any Christian who may have been entangled in this world's prevalent marital disorder before becoming a Christian.

In what I have written the reader will find much repetition in phraseology and in the use of certain Scriptures. The structural order and exhaustive character of the treatise is responsible for this. Furthermore, many will find things new to them and contrary to their former beliefs, feelings, and practice. Therefore, I ask that this writing be read with an open and unbiased mind and all be tested by the Word of God. I myself have been careful to state Scripture for every assertion and inference of a fundamental nature that I have made.

W. Fisher-Hunter

Waynesboro, Pa., U. S. A.—1951.

CHAPTER ONE

CONTENTS

Marriage According to Scripture

CHAPTER ONE

Marriage According to Scripture

The idea that marriage is made in heaven is false. The truth is, marriage is a divine institution that pertains only to the earthly existence of mankind (Matt. 22:30). As constituted in the beginning it is a contract which one man and one woman voluntarily enter into; nevertheless God will hold them responsible in it.

Moreover, the idea that God is responsible for having united every man and woman who are married is also untrue. Doubtless, such an idea has been deduced from the Lord's words, "What therefore God hath joined together, let not man put asunder," Mark 10:9). When these words are interpreted in the light of their contexual setting it will be found that the Lord is not speaking, of the ceremony in the ordinance of marriage, but rather with the institution of it. The use of the word "what" rather than whom confirms this.

The Scriptures directly connected with the constitution of marriage may be divided into three groups: (1) that which is connected with Adam in the beginning (Gen. 2:18, 21-24) ; (2) that spoken by the Lord Jesus to the nation of Israel and His disciples (Matt. 19:4-8) ; and (3) that written by the apostle Paul to the church at Ephesus (Eph. 5:31). When these three portions of Scripture are rightly divided and correctly interpreted in the light of divine purpose and their dispensational setting, there will be no room for doubt as to the mind of God on the matter of divorce and remarriage among Christians.

11

THE ORIGINAL CONSTITUTION AND
DESIGN OF MARRIAGE

"And the Lord God said, It is not good that the man should be alone; I will make him an help meet for him. And the Lord God caused a deep sleep to fall upon Adam, and he slept; and he took one of his ribs, and closed up the flesh instead thereof; and the rib, which the Lord God had taken from man, made he a woman, and brought her unto the man. And Adam said, This is now bone of my bones, and flesh of my flesh; she shall be called woman, because she was taken out of man. Therefore shall a man leave his father and his mother, and shall cleave unto his wife; and they shall be one flesh" (Gen. 2:18, 21-24).

These words clearly declare marriage to be a divine institution for man's welfare. And as constituted by God in the age of innocency, it is the voluntary act of one man uniting unto himself one virgin woman to be his wife. The bond formed in this union makes them one flesh and is meant to be permanent throughout both of their lives. Only one thing can dissolve it—death (Mark 10:6-9; Rom. 7:2; I Cor. 7:39).

THE MARRIAGE CEREMONY

Viewed from an earthly, human and social standpoint marriage may be defined as a ceremony initiatory in the establishing of a socially recognized mating union between one man and one woman.

There is no divine legislation in Scripture regarding the mode or procedure of the ceremony to be used in effectuating the state of wedlock. We are safe in saying that the conditions of legal marriage are decided by the prohibitions which the laws of any country impose upon its citi-

12

zens. To the Christian who is guided by the Word of God in all matters pertaining to his beliefs and practices, the marriage ceremony is one of the ordinances of man which he submits to for the Lord's sake (I Pet. 2:13). Man's law may connect the ceremony with a minister of religion and with the magistrate of state. To the Christian both procedures are proper, and according to Scripture he is at perfect liberty to choose which one of the two is best suited to him. Who lawfully officiates at the ceremony or where the marriage contract is made is inconsequential.

While God has not legislated for the procedure of the ceremony of marriage, nevertheless, in Scripture we have glimpses of tribal and national customs found in olden days among the Orientals. Some of these the reader will obtain from the following portions of the Bible: Genesis 24:1-67, the marriage of Isaac to Rebeckah; Genesis 29:15-30, the marriage of Jacob to Rachel and Leah: Ruth 4:9-12, the marriage of Boaz to Ruth. In these examples we see variation which would suggest that there was no uniform rule to be followed. From them also, when taken together, we gather there were two things prominently associated with the marriage ceremony, namely, a covenant of fidelity for life, and a witness. (Proverbs 2:17; Ezekiel 16:8; Malachi 2:14 make reference to these.)

RESTRICTIONS IN MARRIAGE

While no restrictions were attached to the original law of marriage, it would seem there was an oral agreement among the descendants of Seth not to intermarry with the seed of Cain. After the flood we find Abraham insisting that his son Isaac should marry into his own family lineage (Gen. 24:3). Isaac desires the same thing for his son Jacob (Gen. 28:6-9). A restriction similar in nature was

13

divinely legalized in the nation of Israel, who were forbidden to make marriages with certain nations outside the commonwealth of Israel (Deut. 7:3). In addition to this there were priestly, inter-family, and inter-tribal restrictions (Lev. 18:7-17; 20:11; Deut. 27:20, 22, 23; Num. 36:6; Lev. 18:6-18; 21:7, 14). The same thing in principle is found in the writings of Paul to the churches. Believers are forbidden to make marriages with unbelievers (II Cor. 6:14; I Cor. 7:39). Having more than one wife (polygamy) is indirectly condemned and prohibited by the following injunction: "Let every man have his own wife, and let every woman have her own husband" (I Cor. 7:2). Child marriages, common among the heathen, seem also to be frowned upon in I Corinthians 7:36. In addition to all this the privilege of remarriage is allowed only to the widowed (I Cor. 7:38; I Tim. 5:14). Remarriage by a divorced person whose partner still lives is termed adultery (Rom. 7:2; Mark 10:11; Luke 16:18). Under the law of Moses an exception is made in connection with remarriage. According to Deuteronomy 24:1-4, a divorced person was permitted to do so without incurring the guilt of adultery.

GOD'S DESIGN IN MARRIAGE FRUSTRATED

Biblical history shows that man had not been long upon the earth before he deviated from God's standard of marriage by introducing polygamy. It was begun by Lamech, the sixth descendant from Adam, and continued to be common practice among the Patriarchs. (See Genesis 25.6; 28:3-8; 29:23-30.) The sons of Jacob, Exodus 6:15; I Chronicles 4:5; 7:4; the Judges of Israel, Judges 8:30; the Kings of Israel, I Kings 11:3; II Samuel 12:8; II Chronicles 24:3; and the children of Israel in general, I Samuel 1:2. By the time of Christ it had become rare among Jews.

14

THE PERMANENCY OF THE FIRST LAW OF MARRIAGE

Some may suppose that marriage, being instituted in the Edenic age when man was in a state of innocency, was constitutionally affected by the fall of Adam. The fact that polygamy was tolerated and divorce permitted under the law is cited as proof for such a supposition. But, on the contrary, there is abundant scriptural evidence to prove that, notwithstanding Adam's fall and the perverting of the original institution of marriage by his posterity, the mind of God had not altered in regard to the original divine institution which was to be binding on His creatures. Such proof I hope to present for your examination.

MALACHI'S TESTIMONY TO ITS PERMANENCY

The book of Malachi reveals something of the moral conditions of the Jews consequent to their return from Babylonian exile. Married men took heathen wives, and to clear themselves from the charge of polygamy they deceitfully and unscripturally divorced the wives of their youth, justifying their act on the ground that the law permitted divorce. But in chapter two the prophet reveals the attitude of God concerning such conduct. In verse 14 he shows marriage to be a covenant to which God had been a witness, and that divorce by these husbands was a treacherous dealing and therefore marital infidelity inasmuch as the inspired Word goes on to say, "yet is she thy companion, and the wife of thy covenant." In other words, even though you have divorced your wife, yet (emphasis on yet) she remains the wife of your covenant.

On the other hand, many did not divorce their wives but simply married others. They may have used Abraham

15

and Jacob, both of whom had more than one wife, as a cloak to cover their sin of marital disorder. To such the prophet speaks with a few simple, important and weighty words, namely, "And did He not make *one*?" (verse 15). These words are a clear allusion to God's building of Eve and bringing her to Adam. He made only one woman for one man. He was well able to have made three women for one man, for He had the "residue of the Spirit" to do so. "And wherefore one?" asks the prophet. What design had God in giving only one woman to one man? The answer is, "That He might seek a godly seed" or a seed of God (Hebrew), in contrast to the seed of the adulterer and the whore" (Isa. 57:3), which is begotten through one woman having more than one man. Clearly, this passage, penned by the prophet four thousand years after marriage was constituted, would be designed to show that marriage as established by the Creator at the beginning would allow neither polygamy nor divorce.

CHRIST'S TESTIMONY TO ITS PERMANENCY

Look for a moment at the words of the Lord in the gospel according to Mark, chapter 10, verses 2-9: "And the Pharisees came to him, and asked him, Is it lawful for a man to put away his wife? tempting him. And he answered and said unto them, What did Moses command you?" The Lord was wont to answer a question by asking one, and here it would seem that He was seeking to elicit from His questioners the command that Moses had connected with marriage in the beginning. They were no doubt familiar with this for they acknowledged Moses as the writer of the book of Genesis. However, be that as it may, the Lord then quotes to them God's command written by Moses, to which He adds His own command: "So then

16

they are no more twain, but one flesh. What therefore God hath joined together, let not man put asunder." The use of the word "what" by the Lord instead of "whom" indicates that He had the institution of marriage in mind rather than the ceremony connected with it.

An additional command of the Lord in I Corinthians 7:10-11 could only serve further to convince any Christian of the disobedience of which he would be guilty should he contemplate remarriage after divorce. Nor would ignorance of the scripture rule on the matter eliminate the guilt of adultery were he to enter into such a marriage.

PAUL'S TESTIMONY TO ITS PERMANENCY

Lest any should "consent not to wholesome words, even the words of our Lord Jesus Christ, and to the doctrine which is according to godliness" (I Tim. 6:3), I add the words of Paul the apostle as another proof that the first law of marriage is still binding on Christians. In the epistle to the Ephesians he commands husbands to love their wives in the manner and measure that Christ loves His church. He then restates God's command in Genesis 2:24 written by Moses. "For this cause shall a man leave his father and mother, and shall be joined unto his wife, and they twain shall be one flesh" (Eph. 5:31).

"In the mouth of two or three witnesses shall every word be established." The prophet Malachi, the apostle Paul, and the Lord Himself all bear testimony to the original rule of marriage—the one woman and one man becoming one flesh. Is not this emphasis enough that polygamy or marriage by divorced persons does not have the sanction of God?

NOTE A.

I have given God's mind on what constitutes a true and valid marriage. I have also shown with irrefutable evidence that it is binding in its original form and character on the Christian. In case my words should be misunderstood or misconstrued in such a way as to work an unnecessary hardship to any Christian involved in marital disorder, I wish to make it plain that when speaking of the permanency of marriage I have in mind, only a marriage that is valid. Marriages that are not valid can be annuled. The validity of a marriage is decided by the prohibitions any government imposes upon its subjects.

NOTE B.

Unscriptural Ideas in Marriage

While it is irrelevant to the purpose of my writing; nevertheless I deem it profitable to make some remarks on false ideas in marriage. These observations may especially help those who find themselves in marital difficulty through being in what is commonly called a ''mixed marriage''—where a Protestant is married to a Roman Catholic.

UNSCRIPTURAL IDEAS IN MARRIAGE

In stating some of these I shall confine myself to what is found in Christendom, among some corporate bodies who profess to acknowledge the Holy Scriptures to be the inspired Word of God.

The two chief offenders in associating and injecting error into the ordinance of marriage are the Mormon and the Roman Catholic religious organizations. These two

18

systems have one thing in common—both reject the idea that the Scriptures are sufficient in themselves for Christian belief and practice. The Mormans make up for this supposed deficiency by adding the new revelations of Joseph Smith; Roman Catholicism by adding the traditions of men, decreed and promulgated by Church councils and the Popes of Rome.

MORMON IDEA

What this religious body fully believes and teaches about marriage is so varied, confused, and contradictory that one finds it difficult to present a clear and concise statement on the matter.

However, I am safe in saying that their idea of the ideal marriage institution is as follows: Marriage is a relation that is made in heaven, consummated upon the earth, and continued throughout eternity.

According to Mormon doctrine, the highest degree of future glory can only be obtained in the marriage state. Such teaching certainly leaves the great Apostle Paul out in the cold, for as far as we know he died without having been married.

This system speaks much about "celestial marriage" and teaches that it is marriage for eternity as well as for the earth, this term only applies to a "first marriage." A "polygamous marriage" (a second, or third, etc.) is termed a "state" one. This distinction is made to justify polygamy as having divine authority, and at the same time show it to be inferior to "celestial marriage."

In addition to these three terms already mentioned, there will also be found in Mormon writings such expressions as "earthly marriage," "spiritual marriage," "civic marriage," "proxy marriage."

19

When these ideas are compared with the ordinance of marriage as constituted by God in the beginning (Gen. 2:24), and as restated by the Lord Jesus (Matt. 19:4-8), and by the Apostle Paul (Eph. 5:31) it will be clearly seen that they are humanly conceived by minds not subject to the Word of God, and that they are far removed from the scriptural idea of marriage.

ROMAN CATHOLIC IDEA

What this religious system believes, teaches, and has decreed and promulgated about marriage is very plain, dogmatic, and authoritative. They characterize marriage as of two kinds—sacramental and non-sacramental. We shall better understand what a sacramental one is, if we know what a sacrament is.

They define a sacrament thus: "A sacred sensible sign instituted by Christ in perpetuity to signify grace and to confer that grace on the soul of the recipient."

The essential value this system attaches to its sacraments may be derived from a dogma one of its councils decreed in 1543: "If anyone says that the seven sacraments of the New Law were not instituted by our Lord Jesus Christ, or that there are more or less than seven, namely, Baptism, Confirmation, Eucharist, Penance, Extreme Unction, Order, and Matrimony . . . . let him be anathema."

This same council confirmed this dogma in connection with marriage, in the following words: "Whosoever shall affirm that matrimony is not in truth and properly one of the seven sacraments of the evangelical law, instituted by Christ our Lord, but that it is an invention introduced

other words, the authority and blessing of the church and the presence of a priest are essential in making a marriage valid. And by risking not only a "life of sin" but "living in sin," and being damned forever in hell, can a Roman Catholic dare to get married without the blessing of his church and permission of his priest.

Let us test these high and irrevocable claims by the light of inspired Scripture. The New Testament knows nothing of a universal church (because of inherent or delegated divine authority) having the right to speak for or legislate for all Christians on the face of the earth. Such an usurpation of authority may have been readily acknowledged without question in the dark ages of Christendom when the mass of professing Christians were totally ignorant of the Scriptures of truth, but today the vast majority of professing Christians are enlightened in the Scriptures, and acknowledge the same as being sufficient and their only authority and guide for their beliefs and practices, in ecclesiastical and moral matters. Consequently, all professing Christians outside of the Roman Catholic Church reject its claim that marriage is a church institution, a sacrament, and a matter that it has exclusive and absolute authority over or that the validity of marriage in any way, shape, or form depends upon its decrees, sanction, or blessing.

Protestants look upon marriage as a God-ordained institution, connected with the whole human race (Gen. 2:23-24; Matt. 19:4-6), and a thing unchanged by changing dispensations and conditions. They look upon and accept the ceremony of marriage as an ordinance, seen in Scripture to be always related to civil government.

The reformers of the sixteenth century who restored

22

the Word of God to its proper place and purpose, right-fully rejected the sacramental and mystic theory of marriage and taught that the New Testament treats of it as an established social insitution which the state alone has the right to regulate and determine as well as authorize what is valid and what is not valid.

We do not deny the Roman Catholic religious system the right to issue decrees and state new dogmas for the belief and conduct of its members, but we do object to, and reject its claim to have authority to speak for all professing Christians, and to make its doctrines binding on them.

In the day in which we live the law of the husband has in many countries either been modified or abrogated on the plea that it is barbaric, out-of-date, unworkable, not in keeping with a woman's rights and the equality of sexes. This action on the part of the world is clearly, even though ignorantly, a nullifying of the restrictions which God attached to the woman in her fallen state.

It would seem that in apostolic days some women who believed had the impression their salvation made them free from subjection to their husbands. To correct this false idea and establish the fact that the law of the husband had not been abrogated for them, the apostle writes as follows: "Likewise ye wives be in subjection to your own husbands: that if any obey not the word, they also may, without the word, be won by the conversation of the wives. For after this manner in the old time the holy women, also, who trusted in God, adorned themselves, being in subjection unto their own husbands: Even as Sara obeyed Abraham, calling him lord" (I Pet. 3:1, 5, 6). The apostle Paul also instructed them in like manner. (See Ephesians 5:22-24; Colossians 3:18.)

Thus we see clearly that the dispensation of grace and the receiving of salvation do not effect a change in the Christian woman's place of subjection to her husband, even though he be an unbeliever. Furthermore, the apostle's words show that the rule to be followed by Christian women in the marital relation is not that of the world but rather that of the Scriptures and the example of Sarah (Gen. 18:2), Hannah (I Sam. 1:15), and other holy women who acknowledged the lordship of their husbands, calling them lord.

LAW OF THE HUSBAND TAUGHT
BY THE LORD JESUS

In Mark, chapter 10, verse 12, the Lord Jesus says, "And if a woman shall put away her husband, and be married to another, she committeth adultery." Now a woman putting away her husband is absolutely foreign to the teaching and principle of the law of the husband. Nor did she have the right to do so under the law of Moses. Neither was it common practice among the heathen. But here the Lord, in His omniscience, anticipates the time when the law of the husband would be disregarded, and He teaches that, not withstanding this, the law of the husband is still in effect, and that should any woman divorce her husband she is still unreleased from his authority. The fact that remarriage by her while he is yet alive would constitute her an adulteress (Rom. 7:2), is the tangible proof that her first marriage tie is unbroken.

THE LAW OF THE HUSBAND TAUGHT
BY PAUL THE APOSTLE

Paul in writing to the church at Corinth on marital matters states the same fact in the following words: "The wife is bound by the law as long as her husband liveth; but if her husband be dead, she is at liberty to be married to whom she will: only in the Lord" (I Cor. 7:39). Note, that she is bound during the whole of her husband's lifetime; not until he commits adultery or deserts her or divorces her, but for as long as he lives. Furthermore, the lifetime binding character of the law of the husband is also implied in verse 11 of the same chapter where we read, that if a woman depart from her husband she must remain unmarried, or be reconciled to him. Why remain

27

pgs missing here.

CHAPTER THREE

CONTENTS

Divorce According to Law of Moses

Divorce According to the Law of Moses

Every truth has its doctrine, that is what it teaches. We shall now properly begin the study of what the Scriptures teach on the subject of divorce.

The first time we meet with divorce in Scripture is in the book of Genesis, chapter 21, where we have Abraham sending Hagar, his secondary wife out of his house. There is reason to believe that divorce was common practice among his descendants while they resided in Egypt.

At the time when Moses was made to be a leader over Israel he found that men at their will and pleasure were putting away their wives and marrying others. This was being done seemingly with no recourse to civil law. Therefore, to stop this lawlessness and to restrain men in their sinful behavior, Moses, because of the hardness of their hearts, circumscribed and legalized divorce. It was a protective measure for the bethrothed woman in that it prevented her husband from putting her away at his pleasure. He was thus left only one reason for divorce— the sin of fornication. (See chapter 5 for exact meaning of fornication). Such legislation would also retard fornication and cause unmarried women to value and preserve their virginity, knowing that the loss of it in the unmarried state might be the cause of their becoming the subjects of divorcement.

STATUTE OF DIVORCE

The statute of divorce is found in Deuteronomy 24:1 and is as follows: "When a man hath taken a wife, and married her, and it come to pass that she find no favour

lation of the Hebrew word "ervah," which is the identical Hebrew term used in forty-nine other passages in the Old Testament, always for the word, "nakedness;" forty-seven times in connection with persons and twice to describe the land of Egypt (Gen. 42:9, 12). In Deuteronomy 23:14 it is also incorrectly translated "uncleanness." In both of these occurrences where the term "ervah" is mistranslated "uncleanness," Mr. Newberry gives the proper rendering in the words, "matter of nakedness." In Leviticus 20:11 the word "nakedness" is associated with a prohibition in relation to a man and stepmother; thus: "And the man that lieth with his father's wife hath uncovered his father's (ervah) nakedness: both of them shall surely be put to death." The exact meaning of the term ervah is "nudity" and figuratively may be connected with some disgrace. When the cause for divorce, "some uncleanness," is interpreted in the light of its true scriptural meaning (nudity) and its use in Leviticus 20:11 is considered, it surely is not unreasonable to connect it with sexual intercourse and a woman losing her virginity. The dishonor attached to one losing her maiden character in the unmarried state is a known disgrace the world over.

However, some find it difficult to believe that the term "uncleanness" (Hebrew ervah; English "nudity") implies fornication because they wrongly suppose that (1) the penalty for all cases of fornication was death, and (2) because the woman divorced on account of uncleanness (fornication) *was not put to death*. A help in removing this obstacle is found in Deuteronomy 22 which records different types of fornicators, some of whom were put to death and others who were not.

FORNICATORS WHO WERE PUT TO DEATH

The Whore Type

Type one is found in Deuteronomy 22:13-21 where we have the supposed case of a woman who during the period of her bethrothal had secretly committed fornication of an aggravated type while in her father's house. When the time came for her espoused husband to take her home, and to consummate the marriage union, she was revealed in her true moral character, that of a whore (v. 21). He finds "some uncleanness" in her, or in other words, he discovers that he is not marrying a virgin as he had expected. Legal steps are then taken to have the marriage annulled. His charge, if proved to be true, makes her subject to death by stoning, provided, of course, she is not a fornicator of the type that was exempt from the death penalty.

The Unfaithful Wife

Type two is found in verses 23 and 24 where we have the case of a virgin who is espoused to an husband and becomes unfaithful to him through voluntary fornication with another man. Her breach of the first part of the marriage convenant having come to light by being taken in the act, no question of divorce arises; she is put to death.

These two cases of fornication are looked upon as though the sin had been that of adultery due to the fact that they had taken place during the betrothal* period. Therefore, both incur the same degree of punishment as that of adultery committed in the established marriage relationship. The carrying out of the death penalty under the law was always contingent upon the establishing of guilt by adequate testimony. (Deut. 17:6).

* See Leviticus 19:20 for an exception to this rule.

who treated their espoused wives in such a manner. Nevertheless, it was their right under the law.

These last two instances of fornication substantiate our assertion that under certain conditions fornication did not carry the same degree of guilt, nor merit the same measure of punishment as unfaithfulness during the betrothal period or after they had actually come together in marriage. However, there is one exception to this law in Leviticus 21:9 where the daughter of a priest, guilty of fornication in the unbetrothed state is burned to death.

THE CUSTOM OF MARRIAGE IN ISRAEL

Some find it difficult to accept "fornication" as the only legitimate ground for divorce in Israel because they wrongly believe that all fornication, like adultery, was a capital offence. A knowledge of the marriage ordinance in Israel helps to remove this difficulty. Stated simply and briefly, marriage was a covenant of two parts; the first being the betrothal period and the second, the established marriage state. The betrothal period was of a very binding nature, for during this time they are legally looked upon as a married couple—she is called a "neighbor's wife" and he "her husband" (Deut. 22:23, 24; Matt. 1:20-24). So binding was the betrothal stage that sexual unfaithfulness by the espoused wife in this period was equivalent to conjugal infidelity in the established marriage period. Indeed, both acts are classified alike and both carry the same degree of guilt and merit the same measure of punishment (Deut. 22:21-24; Lev. 20:10). Furthermore, these two cases of marital unfaithfulness must not be confounded with fornication committed in the unbetrothed relation, or in the case where the espoused woman was raped or seduced (Deut. 22:25-29; Exod. 22:16, 17).

37

CUSTOM OF DIVORCE IN ISRAEL

Divorce as practiced in the English speaking world is different than it was in Israel. Because of the fact that we practice no binding betrothal period, it is confined entirely to the established marriage relation. However, in Israel it could take place also during the betrothal period and in some cases in the established marriage if such were not a valid one, but never in a valid established state of marriage where even children might be involved. In verification of this I refer to Deuteronomy 22, verses 19 and 29 respectively. In each of these verses we have the words, "he may not put her away all his days." A glance at the context where these words are found will reveal that they are a prohibition against a man divorcing his wife after they had come together in marriage if she was found to be a virgin at the time. Another reason as proof that divorce was not connected with a valid established marriage relation is the fact that the act of unfaithfulness committed after the marriage had been consummated was a capital offence in Israel, not ground for divorce (Lev. 20:10). The carrying out of this punishment was contingent upon adequate testimony. (Deut. 17:6).

It is during the betrothal period or prior to it that a damsel is involved in the act Scripture terms "fornication," and which, at some future time would become the cause for her betrothed husband divorcing her. (Such cases of fornication are mentioned in Deuteronomy 22:25-29; Exodus 22:16 in which no faithfulness is involved and therefore may be subjects of divorcement). No doubt it was only the hard-hearted who took such action against their espoused wives.

SUSPECTED ADULTERY

We are not to suppose the law made no provision for the establishment of guilt where there was insufficient evidence to carry out the judgment of the law. Numbers chapter 5 v. 11-31 shows that where a husband suspected his wife of marital unfaithfulness without having tangible proof he could have recourse to "the law of jealousies" in order to establish guilt or innocence. If guilt were proved, there is no mention of the husband having the right to divorce. Rather is the woman visited with a special judgment from God which would cause a premature death.

THE SCRIPTURAL EXAMPLES OF DIVORCE UNDER THE LAW

The first example of a man seeking to divorce his wife is in Deuteronomy 22:13-21, which I partially quote: "If a man take a wife and go in unto her, and give occasion of speech against her, and bring up an evil name upon her, and say I took this woman, and when I came unto her, I found her not a maid." One can readily see that the ground for divorce in this instance is premarital unchastity. The husband thinking he was marrying a virgin learned upon taking her unto himself that he had been deceived. But verses 15-21 show that the woman's parents could contest the divorce action. Should the husband's charge be proved false, then he was emerced one hundred shekels of silver and commanded to take her as his wife and forbidden to put her away all the days of his life. On the other hand, should the husband's charge be found true, the woman is stoned to death, not because she was not a maid but on account of her sin having the character of unfaithfulness to an espoused husband. Had the unchastity

39

been connected with rape, seduction, or a simple act committed in the unbetrothed state she would not have been put to death but could be put away by a legal divorce.

The second example of a supposed case for divorce under the law is found in Matthew 1:18-20. Here we have a man seeking to avail himself of the privilege in the law to put away his espoused wife, supposing that she had become unfaithful to him during their time of betrothal. But while he thought over the matter, "Behold the angel of the Lord appeared unto him in a dream saying, Joseph, thou son of David, fear not to take unto thee Mary thy wife: for that which is conceived in her is of the Holy Ghost.' Behold, in the case of Mary a new thing under the sun had taken place. In her case neither uncleanness nor unfaithfulness was involved and therefore, no scriptural ground for divorce existed.

Surely it will be acknowledged that in these two scriptural examples of supposed cases of divorce under the law (either false or true, as the case may be in Deuteronomy 22:13-21, or absolutely unnecessary as in the case of Matthew 1:18-20) the charge or ground in both cases were one and the same; namely, the prenuptial sin of fornication, and not adultery.

MOSAIC STATUTE OF DIVORCE INTERPRETED
BY THE LORD

Scripture is its own best interpreter. Frequently the New Testament throws light on and interprets an Old Testament passage. I am convinced that the Lord Jesus in Matthew 5:32 and 19:9 is doing this very thing in respect to the statute of divorce as given by Moses.

It is well known that when the Lord entered upon His

40

public ministry in Israel He found misunderstanding, error, perversion, and abuse connected with divorce. But His words, "Whosoever shall put away his wife, except it be for fornication, and shall marry another committeth adultery:" removed the misunderstanding, corrected the error, and gave the law of divorce its true interpretation and proper meaning. By such words He plainly tells that it is only for the sin of fornication *(porneia)* and not adultery *(moichao)* that a man can put away his wife. To say that the word "fornication" used here by the Lord means adultery is tantamount to saying that He added to the law by making adultery an additional cause for divorce. It will be readily admitted that adultery, under the law of Moses, was not ground for divorce. Would, then, the Lord who condemned the Pharisees for adding to the law, do that of which He was accusing them? One would hesitate to suggest such a thing, and yet that is exactly what He would have been doing had He told them adultery, committed after a man and woman had actually come together in marriage, was ground for divorce.

SUMMARY

To recapitulate: As stated in the introduction to this treatise, one of the reasons I had in writing was to show from the Word of God that fornication (not adultery) was the only legalized and legitimate cause for divorce in Israel. The establishing of this as a scriptural fact is very important, yea vital, and for the following three reasons: (1) In knowing that fornication (not adultery) constituted the ground for divorce in Israel there is found a key to unlock the Lord's words in Matthew 5:32 and 19:9, the only other places in Scripture where cause for divorce is given. (2) For although Christians are divided on the

41

question of divorce, generally speaking the cause of contention is the term "fornication." Some contend it means every kind of illicit indulgence including adultery; others limit the scope of its meaning to sexual intercourse committed in the unmarried state. (3) Because one of the proofs I shall present as evidence against a Christian having the right to divorce his wife will be the fact that the Lord used the term "fornication" in Matthew 5:32 and 19:9 rather than the term "adultery" when stating the ground for divorce.

Note

The "nakedness" of Deuteronomy 24:1, could at least include the following cases in which the law had no penalty:

(a) Fornication, i,e, pre-betrothal sexual license, not realised on the marriage night and hence not falling within the limits of Deuteronomy 22:13-21. Since the signs that the girl was not a virgin no longer existed there could be no condemnation on her husband's word alone.

(b) Fornication where a man married a woman knowing that she was not a virgin, but finding later that it was not due to a single act as asserted, but to licentious living.

(c) Fornication (under Jewish custom termed adultery) during the betrothal betrayed by premature birth of baby. The Virgin Mary is a special case of this. If the child had had a human father she would have been an adulteress, not a fornicator, for it was conceived after betrothal (Luke 1:27). But there could have been no penalty—the man not being known—except that under Deuteronomy 22:13-21. Joseph and hence all Israelites obviously had the choice of nullity with the death of the erring girl or of a divorce. (See also Lev. 19:20).

Adultery belongs to established marriage
Fornication to pre-marital state

CHAPTER FOUR

CONTENTS

The Words of the Lord Jesus on Divorce and Remarriage Characteristically Considered

The Words of the Lord Jesus on Divorce and Remarriage Characteristically Considered

The Lord Jesus has spoken fully and definitely on the irregularity of divorce: (1) in relation to the institution of marriage in general (Mark 10:6-9); (2) as regarding the Nation of Israel (Matt. 5:32; 19:9); (3) to His disciples (Mark 10:11, 12); (4) in reference to the Kingdom of God (Luke 16:18); and (5) in commandment to His Church (I Cor. 7:10, 11.)

Before we can hope for a uniform regulation on the matter of divorce and remarriage among Christians, these five distinct statements first must be interpreted according to their divine design, always making the contextual and dispensational setting the first law of interpretation and ever bearing in mind what had at all times been God's way—a progressive revelation of truth.

FOUR UTTERANCES OF THE LORD

Of all that the Lord may have had to say respecting divorce and remarriage Scripture records only four instances of His dealing with the subject: Matthew 5:3,32; 19; 9; Mark 10:6-9; 11,12; Luke 16:18. Each of these occasions took place independently of the other, at different times and in different places. The Matthew passages permit a man under the law to divorce and remarry for the cause of fornication; whereas the Mark and Luke passages make no allowance for divorce and positively state in unqualified language that for a divorced person to remarry is an act of adultery. Moreover it is very significant that neither

45

Mark nor Luke make any mention of the Lord's utterance on divorce recorded in Matthew 5:31, 32. Furthermore, when Mark narrates the Lord' utterance on divorce recorded in Matthew 19:3-9, he omits verse 9 which contains the permission to divorce on the ground of fornication.

Now there must be adequate reason for these passages in Matthew which permit divorce being omitted in Mark and Luke, the more so as a knowledge of Matthew in any local Church in the 1st and 2nd cent. down to 1500 A.D. cannot be presupposed. There are only two valid explanations. Either Gentiles would not have understood them, or they applied specifically to the Jewish circumstances of the hearers, or both. There are, of course, characteristic differences to be found in these four sayings, many reasons for which could be cited, but I shall confine myself to one of these, namely, divine design in writing.

Modern Biblical scholars freely acknowledge that by divine design the book of Matthew was written with the Jewish reader in mind; whereas the Gospels of Mark and Luke were written primarily for Gentile readers. This partly accounts for the teaching in Matthew which would permit men under the law to divorce their espoused wives and remarry without incurring the guilt of adultery. Whereas, Mark and Luke record the Lord's statements on the matter which give no cause for divorce and which emphatically state the fact that remarriage by a divorced person or marriage to a divorced person is an act of adultery. How shall we account for this difference in teaching? Some have said that both of these divergent teachings are in agreement and that both are equally applicable to the Christian. They justify this assumption and explain it by the principle that the lesser statement is included in the fuller one.

46

It is true that some differences in the gospel narratives may be explained by this rule. But such a rule cannot be made to operate in this case for the simple reason that they are four distinct and independent utterances. The solution of the difference lies in the acknowledgment of the fact that these two passages in Matthew are simply a proper interpretation of the Mosaic statute of divorce made by the Lord to correct the loose views and false interpretations the Jews attached to it. Whereas, those in Mark and Luke present teaching (not new) based on marriage as originally constituted by God, which makes no allowance for divorce and remarriage.

I submit to the thoughtful consideration of my readers this distinction in the design, the meaning and the use of the words of the Lord Jesus on the matter of divorce and remarriage. I believe it to be the "rightly dividing the Word of Truth" (II Tim. 2:15). When this is acknowledged and acted upon the confusion that now exists in the matter will be eliminated and there will be found one uniform rule for dealing with divorce and remarriage in this present age. And that rule can be none other than no divorce and no remarriage of divorced persons or marriage to divorced persons. It is my purpose now to take up these four utterances separately in order that I may clearly establish my claim that a difference of vital importance exists between these two parts of Scripture.

FIRST UTTERANCE MATTHEW 5:31,32

"It hath been said, Whosoever shall put away his wife, let him give her a writing of divorcement. But I say unto you, That whosoever shall put away his wife, saving for the cause of fornication, causeth her to commit adultery:

47

and whosoever shall marry her that is divorced committeth adultery."

A knowledge of the moral and social conditions that existed in Israel when these words were uttered is helpful in the understanding of their meaning and the reason for their having been spoken. One statute of the law that was greatly abused, misinterpreted and perverted was that which dealt with divorce.

THREE SCHOOLS OF THOUGHT AND PRACTICE

Three schools of thought and practice existed in the nation on the matter. One of these which I shall term the "old school" believed and practiced divorce according to the letter of the law—only on the ground of the sin of fornication. This school is represented by Joseph in the matter of divorce and by John the Baptist in the matter of remarriage. Joseph in ignorance as to what had happened to his espoused wife, through the Holy Ghost, would have divorced her on the ground of premarital unchastity. "But while he thought on these things, behold, the angel of the Lord appeared unto him in a dream, saying, Joseph, thou son of David, fear not to take unto thee Mary thy wife: for that which is conceived in her is of the Holy Ghost." As neither uncleanness nor unfaithfulness were involved in Mary's case there was no ground for divorce; therefore, Joseph took Mary to wife. This example of Joseph and Mary, together with the example of divorce found in Deuteronomy chapter 22 verses 13-21, clearly and unmistakably prove that divorce under the law was connected with the espousal stage of marriage rather than with established valid marriage.

Herod Antipas, who was of Jewish faith, had broken

the law on at least two points: (1) by coveting another man's wife (Exod. 20:17), and (2) by marrying a woman, who was his brother Phillip's wife and his own niece (Lev. 18:16).

John the Baptist's stinging rebuke to Herod plainly shows that notwithstanding, the Jews had relaxed the law in regard to prohibited marriages, nevertheless, the restrictions of the law were still applicable to those under it and should have been enforced in his time.

Another school by the name of Shammai believed that adultery committed in the established marriage relation was a ground for divorce and remarriage. This class subsituted divorce as a penalty for adultery in lieu of the law's judgment for it—death. They were thus allowed to remarry without being stigmatised as adulterers. But who gave the teachers in Israel permission to alter the law or add to it by allowing adultery to be a cause for divorce? It was to rebuke and prevent this very thing that Malachi, one of God's last prophets to Israel said, "Remember ye the law of Moses my servant, which I commanded unto him in Horeb for all Israel, with the statutes and judgments" (Mal. 4:4). Furthermore, who gave the judges in Israel the authority to set aside the death penalty for the convicted adulterer? These teachers and judges may have reasoned that they were doing the next best thing as a substitute for failing to carry out the letter of the law. But God does not recognize any substitute for obedience to His Word. In substance these leaders in Israel, unwilling to terminate an established marriage by capital punishment which was what the law demanded when a wife had committed adultery, resort to the device of making adultery a cause for divorce in order to give freedom to remarry.

49

Is it not significant that the leaders of Israel were ready enough to appeal to the law of Moses as their authority for carrying out the death sentence when it came to passing judgment on the Lord Jesus, on Stephen, and on the woman who was taken in the act of adultery? (John 19:7; 8:5; Acts 7:54-59.

The third school (Hillel by name) believed that divorce could be obtained for any cause whatsoever. Now although confining the ground to one reason—that of adultery—be perhaps a higher standard morally than that of the last mentioned class which allows divorce for any cause, yet both are unscriptural.

In seeking to correct those who perverted the statute of divorce the Lord says, "It hath been said, Whosoever shall put away his wife, let him give her a writing of divorcement" (v. 31). Here the Lord is not quoting Scripture, but rather a saying that was current among the Jews. He did not say, "It is written" or "Moses said." The saying is scripture perverted by the Rabbis to justify adding adultery and many other causes to the one and only legalised ground—namely, the sin of fornication.

It will help greatly in the understanding of Matthew chapters 5, 6, 7 if it be seen that the Lord Jesus is not spiritualizing, changing, abrogating or adding to the law, but rather is he contrasting His doctrine with the teaching of the Rabbis that was then current among the Jews.

The Lord continues with, "But I say unto you." By the use of these words we are not to suppose He was speaking with an authority that set aside the law. He came not to destroy the law. Although His teaching superseded the teaching of the law, yet He never added to the law. On the contrary, He rebuked those who did so. The Lord was simply contrasting His authority as a God-sent

50

prophet with that of the teachers in Israel, whom He had just quoted (v. 31) and whom He had shown to be perverters of the law on the matter of divorce. Then the Lord adds, "That whosoever shall put away his wife, saving for the cause of fornication, causeth her to commit adultery: and whosoever shall marry her that is divorced committeth adultery" (v. 32). By these words the Lord did three things: (1) He gave the statute of divorce, perverted by the teachers in Israel, its true interpretation and proper design; namely, that divorce under the law is strictly limited to one cause—fornication, consequently, all other causes are unscriptural; (2) He states that all who divorce their wives for any other cause than fornication are partakers in the future guilt of such should they remarry; and (3) He stigmatised as adulterers all who marry those illegally divorced under the law of Moses. I say illegally, for persons divorced for fornication were free to remarry without incurring the guilt of adultery. (See Deuteronomy 24:1-4.)

SECOND UTTERANCE LUKE 16:18

"Whosoever putteth away his wife, and marrieth another, committeth adultery; and whosoever marrieth her that is put away from her husband committeth adultery."

This statement on divorce and remarriage was made two years after His first recorded utterance. It seems totally disconnected in the passage where it is found, and it appears difficult to find a cause for its being spoken.

The cause and connection I believe to be as follows: Jesus had spoken in parabolic language of an unjust steward who had been deposed of his stewardship because of his unfaithfulness. The parable simply mirrored the

51

leaders in Israel who had been unfaithful stewards in the things of God committed to their trust, and who were about to have their stewardship taken away from them.

Listening to the parable were the Pharisees who as a sect laid first claim to being the custodians of the law and the upholders of its authority, but who in reality were unfaithful in these for the sake of earthly gain, public place, and the esteem of men. The Pharisees seem to sense that the parable was directed against them, and this may account for their deriding the Lord and making light of His teaching. No doubt they said in their hearts, ''Who gave you authority to bring in new teaching? We recognize no teaching but that of Moses and the Prophets.'' Whereupon the Lord makes this important and pivotal statement, ''The law and the prophets were until John: since that time the kingdom of God is preached, and every man presseth into it.'' These words clearly show that the authority and teaching of the kingdom of God supersedes that of the law and the prophets. But in case these Pharisees should construe His words to mean that the law was at that time abrogated the Lord adds, ''And it is easier for heaven and earth to pass, than one tittle of the law to fail.'' These Pharisees did not know (at least we know they had previously rejected such a thought, Luke 7:30) that the kingdom of God and the law of Moses as two distinct, and authoritative systems were coexistent and ran concurrently during the lifetime of Jesus on earth which ended at the cross.

Now with all their professed zeal for the law and boasted reverence for its sanctity the Pharisees were the foremost transgressors of it in the matter of divorce. Indeed, just before the Lord spoke this parable of the unjust steward, they had been guilty of winking at and

52

condoning the sin of Herod Antipas in marrying his brother Phillip's divorced wife; a thing the law expressly forbade (Lev. 18:16). All this may have been the reason for the Lord, seemingly without cause, introducing at this time and place (in Herod's jurisdiction) His teaching on divorce and remarriage, to wit: "Whosoever putteth away his wife, and marrieth another, committeth adultery: and whosoever marrieth her that is put away from her husband committeth adultery."

This is kingdom of God doctrine—such teaching was in effect before the law was given. It confirms the doctrine of marriage as given by God in the beginning wherein no provision was made for divorce. Furthermore, the words, "The law and the prophets were until John: since that time the kingdom of God is preached," (v. 16) are so closely related to verse 18 as to make it clearly evident the Lord was implying that His teaching—(kingdom of God) on divorce superceded the teaching of the law. It is this doctrine in contrast to Moses' doctrine that is the rule for the conduct of the Christian. This assertion is confirmed by the preaching of Philip (Acts 8:12) and of Paul (Acts 19:8; 20:25; 28:23). Both preached the kingdom of God in contrast to preaching the law of Moses.

THIRD UTTERANCE MATTHEW 19:3-9

"The Pharisees also came unto him, tempting him, and saying unto him, Is it lawful for a man to put away his wife for every cause? And he answered and said unto them, Have ye not read, that he which made them at the beginning made them male and female. And said, For this cause shall a man leave father and mother, and shall cleave to his wife: and they twain shall be one flesh? Wherefore they are no more twain, but one flesh. What

53

therefore God hath joined together, let not man put asunder. They say unto him, Why did Moses then command to give a writing of divorcement, and to put her away? He saith unto them, Moses because of the hardness of your hearts suffered you to put away your wives: but from the beginning it was not so. And I say unto you, Whosoever shall put away his wife, except it be for fornication, and shall marry another, committeth adultery: and whoso marrieth her which is put away doth commit adultery."

It is shortly after the second recorded utterance which we have been considering in Luke 16:18 that the Pharisees come with this twofold question which the Lord answers so comprehensively. Let us look at His answer in detail. It is given in two parts: In the *first* part (1) He reminds them of marriage as it came originally from God the Creator to Adam—that in the institution of marriage there is formed a physical unity (one flesh) comprising *one* male and *one* female; (2) He places marriage where it belongs—not connected with any particular dispensation or nation but with the beginning and God's creation, thereby embracing both Jew and Gentile alike; (3) He again brings before them that God commanded man to cleave unto his wife—the very opposite to the practice of putting her away; and (4) He prohibits interference on man's part with the original institution of marriage. The use of the word "what" instead of "whom" would imply that the Lord was speaking of the institution of marriage rather than the ceremony connected with it. In substance, the first part of the Lord's answer would indicate that even though Moses suffered them to give a bill of divorcement, still it did not in any way change that which God had given at the beginning.

54

Second Part of Question

However, the Pharisees, still desiring to tempt Him, question further, "Why did Moses then command to give a writing of divorcement, and to put her away?" In the second part of His answer the Lord places the responsibility for this deviation from the first law of marriage directly on the hardness of man's heart rather than on the failure of the woman. "Moses because of the hardness of *your* hearts suffered *you* to put away *your* wives: but from the beginning it was not so." His use of the words, *you* and *your* show that the statute of divorce was equally applicable to these Pharisees as well as to those to whom it was first spoken.

In effect, in the second part of the answer, He shows divorce was simply a temporary expedient permitted to men under the law and was not meant to apply to any other part of the human race. By His words, "but from the *beginning* it was not so" the Lord states a principle that is of great value to the Christian, and especially today when there is so much perversion attached to the ordinances of God. I refer to assessing God's institutions by their beginning. When this rule is applied to marriage it will be seen that divorce is an innovation—something that is foreign and absolutely extraneous to marriage as originally ordained. Furthermore, applying this rule to divorce it will be seen to be a privilege that belongs only to the dispensation of the law, only to men under the law and a thing which could be obtained only on the ground of fornication.

Now, notwithstanding the fact that the Lord in the first part of His answer (v.v. 4-6) shows that neither man's sin nor Moses' permission to divorce abrogated the

55

original form of marriage; nevertheless, here in the second part (v.v. 7-9) of His answer he does not deny these Pharisees the right to divorce their espoused wives. The differences among Christians on divorce is due in measure to a lack of understanding these two seemingly conflicting parts of Scripture.

It would be a great help in enabling the Christian to see that the Mosaic privilege of divorce does not apply to him if he understood the divine design in the Lord's twofold answer. In the first part making no allowance for divorce and in the second part permitting it to the Pharisees. This variance in teaching is readily clarified when we take into consideration the fact that during the days of our Lord upon the earth the law of Moses was still in effect. The Pharisees acknowledged they were under it, therefore they were entitled to the concession of divorce which was one of its privileges. However, a new dispensation having new authority and new teaching (yet old) connected with it co-existed and ran concurrently with the law at the time the Lord answered the Pharisees' question. The teaching of the new (Christian) era did not allow divorce.

But with these words, "Except it be for fornication" the Lord corrected the loose views many of the Pharisees held on divorce. And by them also He gave the statute of divorce its true interpretation and proper intent—that only for the sin of fornication (not adultery) could a man under the law scripturally put away his wife.

FOURTH UTTERANCE MARK 10:11,12

And He saith unto them, Whosoever shall put away his wife, and marry another, committeth adultery against

56

her: And if a woman shall put away her husband, and be married to another, she committeth adultery.'' These words were spoken in the house very soon after the Lord had answered the Pharisees' questions and his disciples' first query.

THE DISCIPLES' FIRST QUERY OUTSIDE
THE HOUSE

Evidently the disciples were impressed with the Lord's strictness in connection with marriage. So immediately after He answered the Pharisees they say unto Him, ''If the case of the man be so with his wife, it is not good to marry.'' Or in other words, if marriage is so binding as to shut up a man to one living wife for life, and fornication is the only cause for ever being divorced from her one might as well not be married. The Lord's answer to the disciples' first query is recorded in Matthew 19:11, 12.

THE DISCIPLES' SECOND QUESTION
IN THE HOUSE

It would seem that the Lord's twofold answer in Matthew 19:3-9, to the Pharisees, in which He abrogated divorce on the one hand and in which He also made allowance for it as prescribed by Moses, evidently presented a difficulty to the disciples. Did they wonder if he were contradicting Himself? Or were they disturbed as to which part applied to them who were His disciples in contrast to the Pharisees who were Moses' disciples. At any rate when the Lord got through with the Pharisees and enters into the privacy of a house, we read that they ''asked Him again of the *same* matter.'' I take the words, ''again of the same matter'' to imply that they asked Him again

57

about the strictness of marriage that they had just previously queried Him about. The Lord's answer is as follows: "Whosoever shall put away his wife, and marry
another, committeth adultery against her. And if a woman
shall put away her husband, and be married to another,
she committeth adultery," Mark 10:11,12.

How are we to account for such an extreme difference
in teaching? The answer is simple: (1) The Pharisees and
the disciples were under different authorities—one under
that of Moses and the other that of the Lord. (2) When
the divine blessing that a disciple of Christ inherently and
abstractly possesses is compared with that of a man under
the law, it surely ought not to be difficult to understand
why a higher standard in marital matters is expected of
the Christian.

AN IMPORTANT OMISSION

Some may wonder why I have not incorporated all
the Lord's words on divorce which are recorded in Mark
chapter 10, under the heading of the "fourth recorded
utterance." The reason for this is that Mark narrates two
distinct utterances, verses 4-9 being one, and verses 11 and
12 the other. Now verses 4-9 are simply a repetition of the
third utterance recorded in Matthew 19:4-9 with this difference—Mark's account is not so full as that in Matthew.
Mark omits the words, "And I say unto you, Whosoever
shall put away his wife, except it be for fornication, and
shall marry another, committeth adultery: and whoso
marrieth her which is put away doth commit adultery."
The omissions of Scripture as well as the mentions of
Scripture carry significance and should be attributed to
divine design and purpose in the inspired writings. On the

basis of such a deduction we conclude that the omitting of the Mosaic statute of divorce in Mark as well as the recording of it in Matthew are both alike and together another link in the chain of proof and further evidence that divorce belongs only to those under the law of Moses. For it was to those who knew the law that Matthew wrote, whilst Mark's writing was specially designed for Gentile readers who were ignorant of the law, and Jewish national customs.

Gregory Nazianzen (A.D. 330-381) affirmed: "Matthew wrote the wonderful works of Christ for the Jews, Mark for the Romans; Luke for the Greeks; John, a herald who reaches to the very heavens, for all."

Purpose of Mark's writing. "As Matthew wrote to Jewish readers so Mark wrote for Gentile Christian readers. In illustration of this Mark with one exception at the beginning of his gospel practically omits all reference to the Old Testament prophets. Other marks of difference that connect it with Gentile readers are: the word law does not once occur; the genealogy of our Lord is likewise omitted. Other matters interesting to the Jew are likewise omitted; such as references to the Old Testament, and the law of Moses, Matthew 12:5-7. Explanations are given in some places, which the Jews would not require: thus Jordan is a 'river' (Mark 1:5; Matt. 11:6); the Pharisees etc. used to 'fast' (Mark 2:18). Other customs of theirs are described (Mark 7:19); 'the time of the figs was not yet;' at the Passover men 'eat unleavened bread,' and other explanations are given which Jews would not need. From the general testimony from one or other amongst them, there is little doubt but that the gospel was meant for use in the first instance amongst the Gentile Christian readers." Smith's Bible Dictionary.

There is another mention and another omission that is not without significance. Mark only makes mention of the possibility of a woman putting away her husband. Matthew omits all reference to this. Why? Simply because the law did not allow a woman to put away her husband. Mark's making mention of such an irregularity (uncommon among the Jews), is in keeping with the design of his writing, for a woman putting away her husband was common practice among the Gentiles.

THE LORD'S COMMAND TO THE CHRISTIAN ON DIVORCE AND REMARRIAGE

I Corinthians 7:10,11

"And unto the married I command, yet not I, but the Lord. Let not the wife depart from her husband: But and if she depart, let her remain unmarried, or be reconciled to her husband: and let not the husband put away his wife."

I shall say little by way of explanation at this time and place on these two verses of scripture, as they are fully dealt with in chapter seven. The point I wish to make is—the way they are related to the Lord's utterances that are recorded by the Evangelists.

Nowhere in the gospels do we find these words in the exact form that they are given by the Apostle Paul. In all probability they are a maxim based on the teaching of the Lord, taught by the twelve apostles and received by the Christians of the apostolic era as the Lord's ruling for them, on the matter of divorce and remarriage.

This ruling is at complete odds with the words of the Lord recorded in Matthew 5:32 and 19:9, which permit divorce for fornication. However, it is not in disagreement with the Lord's words of Mark 10:6-12; Luke 16:18.

60

SUMMARY

I would restate briefly some of the characteristic differences in the Lord's utterances in the hope that the recapitulation may clarify and help to distinguish vital differences in them. *In the first utterance* (Matt. 5: 31, 32), the Lord Jesus is seen acting in the capacity of a God-sent prophet to Israel, correcting errors and abuses that had become attached to the law of divorce. In doing this He gave the statute of divorce its true interpretation and proper application—that only for fornication (premarital unchastity) was divorce permitted under the law. *The second utterance* (Luke 16 :18), is distinctly related to and connected with kingdom of God authority and teaching. For that reason no cause for divorce is given. Furthermore it specially stresses that marriage to a divorced person is adultery. *The third utterance* (Matt. 19 :4-9, was directly addressed to the Pharisees. It is an answer to their question on what was the legal grounds for divorce under the law. This accounts for the Lord stating that fornication (not adultery) was the only lawful reason for divorce and, at the same time, allowing it for fornication to the Pharisees because they were under the law. *The fourth utterance* (Mark 10 :11, 12), is very closely associated with the third for it grew out of it and has its roots in it: nevertheless, it is in its entirety an independent and distinct saying. It specially stresses that remarriage by a divorced person is adultery. There is also this noteworthy difference—it is the only one spoken privately in a house and exclusively to the Lord's disciples, who were the nucleus of His then future Church. This accounts for no mention of a cause being given as grounds for divorce.

CHAPTER FIVE

CONTENTS

The Words of the Lord Jesus Which Permit Divorce and Remarriage Exegetically Considered

The Words of the Lord Jesus which Permit Divorce and Marriage Exegetically Considered

"But I say unto you, that whosoever shall put away his wife, saving for the cause of fornication, causeth her to commit adultery; and whosoever shall marry her that is divorced committeth adultery" (Matt. 5:32). "And I say unto you, whosoever shall put away his wife, except it be for fornication, and shall marry another, committeth adultery: and whoso marrieth her which is put away doth commit adultery" (Matt. 19:9).

It is universally accepted that these words of the Lord imply divorce and remarriage. Nevertheless, some there are who, while admitting they teach divorce, deny that they imply permission to remarry. Those who contend that remarriage is not included only discredit themselves as reliable expositors of Scripture, and at the same time add to the confusion that already exists on the subject among Christians. Admitting that the Lord's word also denote remarriage in no way adversely affects the assertion—"The Lord Jesus prohibited divorce and remarriage to the Christian."

While I freely admit the Lord's words of Matthew 5:32 and 19:9 allow divorce and remarriage, I emphatically reject the assumption so commonly attributed to them that they teach divorce and remarriage on the ground of adultery committed in the consummated marriage state. Such teaching contains four serious implications. First, it encourages both adultery and divorce, for it amounts to saying, "All one needs in order to qualify for divorce is

63

proved adultery." One has only to search his own heart in order to see that this cause could be easily provided by either party. Secondly, to maintain that the Lord's words permit Christians to divorce on the ground of adultery is to misrepresent Him and to associate His name with the disruptive conditions and evils that follow in the train of divorce. Thirdly, it further follows that to make the Lord's words mean that a Christian has the right to divorce on the ground of adultery committed in the established marriage relation in which even children may be involved is tantamount to charging the Lord with adding to the law of Moses. For it is common knowledge that, under the law, adultery committed in the consummated married state was not a reason for divorce, but rather an offense punishable by death (Lev. 20:10), or by special judgment at the hand of God (Num. 5:11-31). Fourthly, to assert that the Lord gave a Christian the right to divorce and remarry on the ground of adultery is to charge Him with having made contradictory statements and to associate Him with confusion.

MISUSE OF MATTHEW 5:32;19:9

Generally speaking, Christians who take license to divorce and remarry base their claim for doing so on the term "fornication." They contend that it means adultery. But does it? It is also said that the terms "fornication" and "adultery" are synonymous in meaning and are used as interchangeable terms in Scripture. How can these two expressions, which are the English equivalents of two different Greek words (*porneia* and *Moichao*), be the same in meaning? The value in the acknowledgment of the distinction in the meaning and use of these two terms cannot be

64

overestimated. For when it is admitted that the term "fornication" as used by the Lord in Matthew 5:32 and 19:9 does not mean adultery, then it naturally follows that the Christian's case for divorce is lost. He is then without a cause for, as a rule, it is from the teaching of these two verses that he finds authority for his action.

Believing this misconception of words to be chiefly responsible for the confusion that exists on the subject, and for most of the divorces among Christians, I deem it both wise and vital to give abundant scriptural proof that the word "fornication" used by the Lord in connection with divorce does not mean adultery.

MEANING OF THE TERM "FORNICATOR"

Although fornication and adultery are acts similar in nature, yet they are different in relationship and in the degree of guilt attached to them. (See Deuteronomy 22:22, 28, 29) Fornication is the act committed before true marriage has been established, whereas adultery is the act committed in a valid marriage relation.

The Greek word *pornos* occurs only ten times in the New Testament, and is translated "fornicator" twice, "fornicators" thrice, "whoremonger" once, and "whoremongers" four times. The original word signifies to prostitute one's body for a price or for gain. It comes from a root word which signifies "*to sell.*" Thereupon they who commit uncleanness for gain are said to sell their bodies (Ezekiel 16:33, 34); however, it is also used for the same act of uncleanness although no gain be intended or derived from it. This latter aspect would apply to one who commits a simple offense rather than to the person who is termed a whore by reason of continuous trafficking in the act.

65

Unlike adultery, under the law, every type of fornication was not judged as a capital offense. This differential treatment is clearly seen in Deuteronomy chapter 22. In verse 21 we have a fornicator whose marriage is invalidated, and who is put to death because as an unmarried woman she played the whore, committing fornication of an aggravated type. In verses 28 and 29 of the same chapter we have two unmarried persons committing fornication and the penalty for their illicit act is not death. In this latter case the man who wronged the virgin is fined fifty shekels and must take her to wife and never divorce her all the days of his life. (See also Exodus 22:16, 17, for a similar case of simple fornication that did not merit capital punishment.) For the most part it would be women involved in such cases of simple fornication who were the subjects of divorce.

MEANING OF THE TERM "ADULTERER"

The Greek word *moichos* occurs four times in the New Testament and is always translated "adulterers." In Greek the word is connected with the root meaning *"to pass water,"* here *to pass seed."*

The notation of our English word, adultery, is taken from the Latin, *adulterium*, and that from going *ad alterius torum*, another's bed. Thus is Ruben's incestuous adultery described, "Thou wentest up to thy father's bed" (Gen. 49:4). And the adulteress enticeth a young man to her husband's bed (Prov. 7:16-19).

Unlike fornicators, under the law, on the basis of adequate testimony adulterers without exception had to be put to death. (See Deut. 22:22; Lev. 20:10; John 8:5; Deut. 17:6).

DICTIONARY MEANING OF FORNICATION
AND ADULTERY

Although we do not appeal to the work of men to justify the definition of an inspired term, nevertheless, it may be of interest to some to know that such a standard work as Hastings Bible Dictionary defines adultery thus: "It usually denotes sexual intercourse of a married woman with any other man than her husband, or of a married man with any other than his wife. More specifically in Israel as well as Roman law, the term was confined to illicit intercourse of a married or betrothed woman with any other than her husband. Other unchaste relations were disapproved, but they were described by different words. It was deemed an outrageous crime, striking at the laws of inheritance and inflicting a spurious offspring on the husband, and was to be punished by death, Lev. 20:10; 19:20-22; Ezek. 16:38, 49 by the act of stoning John 8:5. A bondmaid was only scourged (Lev. 19:20).

The Century Dictionary and Encyclopedia of English Literature defines fornication and adultery thus: "fornication—the act of sexual intercouse on the part of an unmarried person with a person of the opposite sex whether married or unmarried; "adultery"—violation of the marriage bed; carnal connection of a married person with any other than their married spouse."

Webster's New International Dictionary (2nd ed.) bears similar witness when it states and defines fornication thus: "fornication—illicit sexual intercourse between a man and a woman that does not by law amount to adultery. Fornication is sometimes, especially in the Bible, used to include all sexual intercourse except between husband and wife or concubine; but is usually distinquished from adultery and somtimes from incest."

DISTINCTION IN THE USE OF THE TERMS "FORNICATION" AND "ADULTERY"

It has been said that fornication is sometimes used in Scripture in such a way as to include adultery. Even if we granted this implication yet such a rule could not possibly be made to apply where fornication and adultery are joined together and distinguished the one from the other; and in many cases both words are used in the same sentence. (See Matthew 5:32; 15:19; 19:9; I Corinthians 6:9; Galatians 5:19; Hebrews 13:4 R.V.).

DISTINCTION SEEN IN THE LORD'S WORDS

The Lord differentiated between these two terms. In Matthew 15:19, when listing the self-defiling elements a person had within his own heart, He mentioned fornication and adultery as two different and distinct uncleannesses. And in Matthew 5:32 and 19:9, when stating the only cause a man under the law had for putting away his espoused wife, He used the term fornication to describe it. Why fornication? Why not adultery? The reason for the difference and the use of fornication is: The legitimate cause for divorce under the law is created by the woman committing illicit sexual intercourse while she is in the unestablished marriage relation.

Now in the same verse the Lord uses the term adultery, but not in connection with divorce, but rather with the remarriage of a divorced person, or marriage to an illegally divorced person. Why did he not use the term fornication when speaking of the remarriage of unlawfully divorced persons or marriage by others to such persons, if the two terms are synonymus in meaning? The reason adultery is used in this connection is: The scripture supposes the person who remarries is still in the established married bond owing to her divorce having been procured for some cause other than the only lawful one—fornication. Death only dissolves a *scripturally constituted* marriage union,* but divorce under the law could disannul the marriage contract of two persons who had been espoused if the woman were found not to be a virgin when the time came to consummate the marriage union. The reason for adultery being used in the case of the man who marries the woman put away is: She is divorced for some cause other than fornication and therefore still in the marriage bond. In such a case the use of the word fornication would have been out of order for fornication properly describes the sinful act committed by unmarried persons.

It should be quite obvious to the careful reader of scripture that the Lord is not condemning remarriage of persons or marriage to persons who have been divorced for the cause of fornication. The law of divorce allowed divorced persons to remarry without incurring the guilt of adultery. (See Deuteronomy 24:1-4; Leviticus 21:7.) It is equally clear the Lord is condemning remarriage of persons divorced for some cause other than fornication—be that cause adultery, desertion, incompatibility, cruelty, etc.

Paul's use of the word adulteress in a similar connection ought to put an end to the controversy on the matter. We read in Romans 7:2, 3, "For the woman which hath a husband is bound by the law to her husband so long as he liveth: but if the husband be dead (not when he commits adultery against her), she is loosed from the law of her husband. So then if, while her husabnd liveth she

* The conditions of legal marriage are decided by the prohibitions which the laws of any country impose upon its citizens.

be married to another man, she shall be called an adulteress: (not a fornicator) but if her husband be dead, she is free from that law; so that she is no adulteress, though she be married to another man."

Search the Scriptures from their beginning to their end and it will be found that there are only two classes of persons who may legitimately remarry without incurring the guilt of adultery. One class, those who were legally divorced under the law. Deuteronomy 24:1-4; Leviticus 21:7; Matthew 5:31; 19:9. The other class is the widowed, be he Jew or Christian (I Cor. 7:39).

DISTINCTION SEEN IN THE PHARISEE'S WORDS

Even the Pharisees understood that the two terms "fornication" and "adultery" were distinctly different in their meaning and use. In John chapter eight, we have them making the discrimination to convey two acts of a similar nature. In verse 4, they say, "This woman was taken in adultery." Again in verse 41, they say, "We be not born of fornication." In the case of the woman, they use the term adultery for she was in the married relation when she committed the act of unfaithfulness. Her case is described in Deuteronomy 22:22. The Pharisees knew this and asked that the penalty of the law be carried out and the woman stoned to death. But in their controversy with the Lord over His origin, relationship and birth, they use the term "fornication" for they ignorantly and wickedly suppose that He was born out of wedlock. Their words "Where is thy father?" (John 8:19) would indicate this.

DISTINCTION SEEN IN PAUL'S WORDS

The same distinction in the use of the terms is found in the writings of Paul the Apostle. In 1 Corinthians 6:9-11, when describing the moral character of some of the saints prior to their conversion, he makes a distinction in saying some had been "fornicators" and some had been "adulterers." In chapter five of the same book, we have the case of a man who had illicit relations with his "father's wife," and Paul terms the sin that of fornication. Why did he not call it adultery? Simply because the evil doer was having illicit relations with one so near of kin as to bring the act into the category of incest. In such a case even if a marriage relation existed it would not be a valid one. Hence the illicit sexual intercourse is properly described as fornication.

Again in the First Epistle to the Corinthians, in answer to a question as to whether it is more beneficial to be unmarried than married, we read: "Nevertheless to avoid fornication, let every man have his own wife, and let every woman have her own husband" (7:2). The sin to be avoided here by unmarried persons is fornication. The use of the term adultery in this case would have been out of order and a misuse of words, for adultery is a sin connected with persons in the marriage relation. At this point we ask a self-explanatory question: Why does the apostle advise and give marriage as a remedy and prevention against fornication if the sin (illicit sexual act) committed by a married person is fornication? We might as well tell married persons to get divorced in order to avoid fornication and unmarried persons to get married to avoid adultery.

Furthermore, in Galatians the apostle writes, "Now the works of the flesh are manifest which are these: adultery, fornication, uncleanness, lasciviousness," etc. (5:19). It has been said, and it is commonly accepted, that the term "fornication" as used in the New Testament covers all forms of sexual evil. How can an honest and scripturally enlightened mind receive such an assumption in the light of the scripture just quoted, which joins together and distinguishes between four kinds of sexual evil—adultery, fornication, lasciviousness and uncleanness?

Even the writer of the epistle of Hebrews distinguishes between the two terms and in his use of them. In describing two classes of wicked persons, he says, "Fornicators and adulterers God will judge" (Hebrews 13:4; R.V.) The context clearly shows that the writer has the unmarried and the married in mind.

This distinction in the use of these two terms is also seen in the book of the Revelation. In this book "fornication" is used to symbolize the illicit intercourse of the Christian individually and of the Church corporately with the world. As the Church is not yet married to the Lamb, her unfaithfulness is termed fornication (Rev. 2:20-22). In chapter 17:1,2, the false church is symbolized as a great whore and that also is the reason why "fornication" is used to describe her illicit intercourse with the kings and merchants of the earth. Adultery does not properly, illustrate the sexual acts of a whore and that of an unmarried woman.

With regard to the term "fornication" mentioned in Acts 15:20,29. It seems to me that when the local heathen conditions, together with the Holy Spirit's general use of the term are considered, the word should be understood in connection with sexual intercourse prohibited by scripture—in other words committed where no valid marriage existed hence termed fornication.

DISTINCTION SEEN IN THE OLD TESTAMENT
Nor is the distinction in the use of the two terms confined to the New Testament. In Ezekiel, the Lord when

72

portraying the unfaithfulness of Israel as a nation and Jerusalem as a city symbolizes them as a woman in the relation of a wife to a husband, in contrast to that of an unmarried whore, saying, "and hast not been as an harlot, in that thou scornest hire; But as a wife that committeth adultery, which taketh strangers instead of her husband" (Ezek. 16:31,32).

Also, in Hosea the same distinction seems more explicit. "I will not punish your daughters when they play the harlot *(commit fornication)* nor your daughters-in-law when they commit adultery" (4:14 New Trans. J.N.D.) The daughters being in the unmarried state, their illicit act is termed fornication. The daughters-in-law being in the married relation their sexual act of unfaithfulness to their husbands is termed adultery.

OBJECTION

I will cite one particular that has been brought forward as proof for including adultery in the term fornication. Paul in the First Epistle to Timothy chapter one, when stating who the law was made for, mentions "fornicators" (R.V.) but omits adulterers. It has been said, this omission is proof that adulterers are included in the term fornicators. But this is specious reasoning. Are there not many more immoral acts not mentioned in this place but for which the law is also made? Is it not much more reasonable to suppose that adultery, although not specifically mentioned, is included in the apostle's words, "And if there be any other thing that is contrary to sound doctrine" (Verse 10).

SUMMARY

Believing the crux in the whole case of a Christian getting a divorce on the ground of adultery is wrapped up in the misuse of one word "fornication" I have gone to great lengths to show that when the term is interpreted in the light of the statute of divorce as given by Moses and by the rule of accumulative evidence, it cannot honestly be made to mean adultery.

Furthermore, in the light of the distinction which Scripture makes between fornication and adultery, one can readily see the wisdom of God and the perfect use of words by the Lord Jesus when He used the term fornication instead of adultery in giving the only scripture cause for divorce. Also, He used the term adultery and not that of fornication to designate remarriage of persons under the law who were divorced for any cause other than the sin of fornication (Matt. 5:32; 19-9). This same rule on remarriage is followed by the Lord in Mark 10:11,12; Luke 16:18 when describing the remarriage of a divorced person; He terms it adultery.

The natural and inescapable conclusion we must accept in the matter is: that the acceptance of the thesis—namely the term "fornication" in Matthew 5:32 and 19:9 does not mean adultery, leaves the Christian without a cause for divorce, for generally speaking his only authority for such action is based on these two verses.

CHAPTER SIX

CONTENTS

The Words of the Lord Jesus Which Permit Divorce and Remarriage Dispensationally Considered

The Words of the Lord Jesus which Permit Divorce and Remarriage

DISPENSATIONALLY CONSIDERED

In consideration of the serious nature of the assertion which I shall presently make—an assertion that concerns the Christian's use of Matthew 5:32 and 19:9, as the basis for his right to divorce, I deem it advisable to make a few prefatory remarks on the necessity of rightly dividing the Word of God.

While it is true that ultra-dispensational teaching has wrought havoc in certain circles of biblically enlightened Christians; nevertheless, it is no exaggeration to say that ignorance of dispensational teaching is one of the root causes of many of the heresies and errors found in Christendom. Nor is it any exaggeration to say that the discovery and proper use of dispensational teaching is the chief factor in the correct apprehension that so many Christians have of the Word of God today.

DISPENSATIONAL TEACHING

From the creation of Adam up to and including the present dispensation, time may be divided into five major periods. A knowledge of the beginning and ending of these is indispensable in order to properly interpret and rightly divide God's Word.

When properly divided it then becomes easy to keep the truth pertaining to each quite distinct. Every dispensation has a distinct line of truth belonging exclusively to it which does not belong to any other.

Not only must the Word of God be rightly divided as to its times and dispensations, but the same must be done as to its truth and teaching. If we take truth which belongs in its application to one dispensation and apply it to another, we shall be in danger of putting scripture at variance with scripture. The practice of misappropriated truth will result in confusion and disruptive consequences. This very condition is found today among Christians on the matter of divorce. *how about variant traditions?*

One thing that marks off a change in dispensations is the introduction of new teaching, which may even seem contradictory to the former one. This in part accounts for those of a passing dispensation being reluctant to receive teaching which might be in opposition to their former instruction. We have this illustrated in Luke chapter five, where the Pharisees murmur at the words of the Lord Jesus. He attributes their conduct to a well-known principle by saying, "No man also having drunk old wine straightway desireth new: for he saith the old is better" (Luke 5:39).

DEVICE OF THE DEVIL

It has been a device of the devil down through the ages to get the Lord's people occupied with and seeking to practice truth that belongs to a past or a future dispensation. He has thus diverted them from doing God's expressed will for them in connection with the dispensation in which they have been living, and created contention and confusion among them. Many Christians have been caught in this very snare in the matter of divorce. Such persons fail to see that: (1) the institution of marriage is not connected with any particular dispensation or nation, and (2) that divorce is related to one dispensation only—

namely the law, and to one people only—namely the nation of Israel, and was permitted for one cause only—namely fornication.

While most Christians who divorce may be honest in the conviction that they are acting according to Scripture; having Scripture for one's conduct is not in itself sufficient nor a safe criterion to warrant its being accepted as a scripturally valid practice for the Christian. For example, a Christian may say, "I do not eat all kinds of meat and my reason for so acting is found in the book of Deuteronomy chapter 14:7,8." Now anyone possessing the faintest ray of dispensational light knows that these prohibitions in respect to eating certain kinds of flesh apply exclusively to the nation of Israel, and that they are truth connected with the dispensation of the law. As proof that they do not apply to the Christian I refer to the words of the Lord Jesus (Matt. 15:10,11); the Apostle Paul (Rom. 14:14; I Tim. 4:3-5); and the vision given to Peter (Acts 10:9-18.)

Generally speaking, Christians who divorce and remarry justify their right to do so by the Word of God. They say, "I have two texts of Scripture as my authority." In most cases the texts alluded to are the words of the Lord Jesus in Matthew 5:32 and 19:9. Now it cannot be gainsaid that these two passages imply permission to divorce and remarry. But there are good reasons for being persuaded that the Christian who uses these two verses of Scripture as his authority for divorce and remarriage is just as guilty of misusing Scripture as he who justifies his not eating certain kinds of meat by the scriptures in the book of Deuteronomy.

THE IMPORTANT ASSERTION

I have previously stated that it is improper for the Christian to believe he has the right to divorce and remarry on the assumption that fornication means adultery. I wish now to go a step further and assert that Christians are not warranted under any circumstances in using Matthew 5:32 and 19:9 as authority for divorcing and remarrying.

Indeed, when all is said and done, it is the misinterpretation and misuse of these two texts of Scripture that is the principal cause for the confusion and lack of oneness of mind among Christians on the matter of divorce and remarriage.

The acknowledgment of the fact that Matthew 5:32 and 19:9 belong exclusively to the dispensation of the law, and are applicable only to men under it, would be a great factor in ending the contention over the practice of divorce.

Furthermore, such an admission would result in another valuable consequence, for then it would be immaterial to the Christian whether the term "fornication" does or does not mean adultery in that the two texts do not apply to him.

However, I am inclined to believe my assertion—the Christian's misuse of Matthew 5:32 and 19:9 as a ground for divorce will not be readily accepted by some. I consider the foregoing assertion the main thesis of all that I write on the subject of divorce, and so vital that it warrants a full and extended explanation, for I anticipate objections.

OBJECTIONS ANSWERED

Some may say, "By relegating these two passages to the Jewish dispensation and making them apply exclusively to men under the law of Moses, are you not setting a precedent that will give others license to do the same thing in principle with other portions of the Word of God in Matthew? Might not others teach that Matthew chapters 5, 6, and 7, apply exclusively to the subjects of the future earthly kingdom of heaven? And might not some say that verse 20 of chapter 18 and verses 19 and 20 of chapter 28 are not for the Christian, but belong to some future dispensation?" The idea of not teaching a truth out of fear of it being misunderstood or abused, is certainly false. Have not many of the privileges and doctrines of Christianity been so treated?

It is very remarkable that many of the contentions and divisions in Christendom have been caused by misappropriations of the teaching of the book of Matthew. I list a few of these misappropriations. Is not the Sermon on the Mount taught to be binding on the Christian; notwithstanding there is much in it that is incongruous with Christian doctrine and untenable in Christian practice? And that some parts of it are at complete variance with the full revelation of Christian doctrine? We admit there are moral principles in Matthew chapters 5-7 which are applicable to the Christian. Matthew 5:32, which deals with the rite of divorce, does not come under this rule on account of it being a legal enactment which was part of the social order of the nation. Have not the following words, "Himself took our infirmities and bare our sicknesses" (Matt. 8:17), been used to support the false theory that there is physical healing for the Christian in the atonement of Christ? Is not the gospel of the kingdom of heaven which has healing the sick and casting out demons connected with it being preached today by well-meaning persons? Many more misappropriations of Matthew's writing could be mentioned.

But it may be said, "Were not these two texts which allow divorce, spoken by the Lord Jesus?" Yes, they were, but it does not necessarily follow that everything spoken by Him applies to this age, or that they should be practiced by the Christians. Furthermore, the determining factor in the interpretation of Scripture must be in the light of its context: namely, it applies first to those to whom it is addressed. The words of Matthew 5:32 and 19:9, were spoken exclusively to Jews who were at that time under the law of Moses. The word "whosoever" in these verses has led some to conclude that the doctrine taught is of universal application. But the word "whosoever" here is governed by the antecedent "you" which restricts the privilege of divorce to those addressed; to wit, the nation of Israel. This personal restriction is further implied in the words, "But I say unto you." The Lord did not use these words on the two other occasions when He spoke on divorce (Mark 10:11,12; Luke 16:18).

Persons skilful in the use of Scripture know and own that the Lord taught many things that were not intended for presentday practice. In comparing Scripture with Scripture we find many words spoken in the gospels that are countermanded in the epistles to the churches, and some times even within the gospel writings themselves.

Take for an example of this, the Lord's commission to the disciples in Matthew chapter 10:1-15, "These twelve Jesus sent forth and commanded them saying, Go not in the way of the Gentiles, and into any city of the Samaritans enter ye not: But go rather to the lost sheep of the house of Israel. And as ye go, preach, saying, The kingdom of heaven is at hand." (vs. 5-7). Do these words apply to Christians? It requires only a meagre knowledge of rightly dividing God's Word to know that they have their applica-

82

tion and fulfillment during the days of our Lord's life upon the earth and before His public rejection by Israel. Let the reader compare this commission of the Lord to His disciples with His commission to them in chapter 28, verses 19 and 20. What is prohibited in the one is countermanded in the other. The last commission revokes the one previously given.

Moreover, the Lord spoke words which applied neither to the age in which He was living nor to the present one. For instance, in Matthew chapter 24, we read, "But he that endureth to the end, the same shall be saved, and this gospel shall be preached unto all nations for a witness; and then shall the end come." When these words are interpreted in the light of their context and the truth of the gospel of the grace of God, it will be found that they are connected with and shall find their fulfillment in a dispensation yet future.

Again, it may be said, "Did not the Lord Jesus, when commanding His disciples (Matt. 28:19, 20) tell them to teach those who were baptized to observe all things whatsoever He had commanded them?" Yes, He did. But notice the wording. It would not include all things they ever heard Him utter. There is a vast difference between all the words He spoke and what He commanded. The teaching was to be confined to what He commanded. Scripture would bear out that these commands were given when the Lord met with His disciples at a mountain in Galilee. The time would have been during the interval that elapsed between His resurrection and His ascension into heaven (Matt. 28:16-20; Acts 1:2). It is taken for granted that what the Lord commanded at the institution of the Lord's Supper would be included in His post-resurrection teachings.

83

EARLY CHURCH CONTENTION

It would seem there were contentions in the church at Corinth on the matter of divorce. No doubt the Jewish believers would want the teaching of the law of Moses to be the sole handbook in the matter. On the other hand, the Gentile believers would desire the civil law of their land to be the regulator. Who was right in the controversy? Both were wrong. The Jewish believer in that he sought to be guided by and practice truth that belonged to the dispensation of the law of Moses. The Gentile believer in not realizing that the doctrine of the apostles was to be the rule and standard for the Christian's life, belief and conduct (Acts 2:42; I Cor. 7:17; 14:37; Ephesians 2:20). Evidently to put an end to the altercation, an appeal is made to Paul the apostle. His inspired authoritative reply is found in I Corinthians 7:10-11, "Unto the married I command, yet not I, but the Lord. Let not the wife depart from her husband, but and if she depart, let her remain unmarried, or be reconciled to her husband, and let not the husband put away his wife."

I draw the reader's attention to a special circumstance which contributes further proof to my assertion that Matthew 5:32 and 19:9 should not be used by the Christian as authority for divorce. I refer to the fact that in answering the Corinthian church's question, the apostle did not direct them to the law of Moses where the statute of divorce is found. Nor did he make mention of the Lord's words found in Matthew 5:32 and 19:9, words that undeniably imply permission to divorce. But on the contrary he quoted the Lord's command which prohibited divorce and remarriage (I Cor. 7:10,11).

In the light of the apostles' answer I would ask a vital

84

question: "Why, in answering the Corinthians, did he not make reference to the Lord's words in Matthew 5:32 and 19:9, where it is plainly stated that divorce is permissible on the ground of fornication?" The answer should be obvious—the apostles knew that the teaching of these two verses which warrant divorce for fornication was Mosaic legislation and therefore applicable only to men under the law. Although they were the Lord's own words, yet they were not His teaching and commandments for His disciples and His Church.

NINE REASONS WHY MATTHEW 5:32 AND 19:9 DO NOT APPLY TO THE CHRISTIAN

I. Because the concession of divorce was given by Moses, and he never legislated for the church. It was a privilege granted to men in Israel. And privileges of the law no more belong to Christians than do the curses and its bondage. Why should the Christian separate the curse from the privilege?

II. Because the Mosaic statute of divorce is properly only suitable and tenable to marriage as practiced by the Jews in ancient days. It was not divorce as we know it today in Christendom. It was simply the annulling of the first part of the marriage covenant and did not apply to the breaking up of an established marriage in which even children may have been involved.

III. Because "hardness of heart" is associated with the giving of divorce. Who would ever unite hardness of heart with a true Christian? This circumstance alone ought to cause every believer to disassociate himself from the divorce evil.

IV. Because the privilege of divorce given by Moses

and restated and properly interpreted by the Lord Jesus belonged only to the male sex. Notwithstanding this we have Christian women divorcing their husbands and using Matthew 5:32 and 19:9 as their authority.

V. Because the term "fornication" does not mean adultery but rather premarital unchastity.

VI. Because Mark when recording the second utterance of the Lord (Mark 10:3-9) omits the words which permit divorce for the cause of fornication (Matt. 19:9). Omissions in Scripture are of divine design. It is generally admitted that the reason for this omission is that Mark wrote for Gentile readers. Nor is it without reason that permission to divorce is found only in the Gospel by Matthew. I believe the reason is: divorce is connected only with the law of Moses and the nation of Israel.

VII. Because Paul the apostle when writing to the church at Corinth on matters pertaining to divorce never used the words of Matthew 5:32 and 19:9, but rather did he quote the Lord's command which prohibited divorce (I Cor. 7:10,11). This command was the rule accepted by the Christians of the primitive churches. It is based on the following Scriptures: Matthew 19:3-8; Luke 16:18.

VIII. Because for a Christian to base his authority to divorce on Matthew 5:32 and 19:9 is to cause contention, create confusion and make void other parts of Scripture that deal with divorce and which are at complete variance with the Matthew passages. (The other parts of Scripture are: Mark 10:11,12; Luke 16:18; I Cor. 7:10, 11.

IX. My final reason for denying the Christian the right to use Matthew 5:32 and 19:9 is: When these passages in Matthew are interpreted by the rule of, *last mention*, it will be found their teaching is abrogated for the Christian and superseded by the following words, "And unto the married I command, yet not I, but the Lord, Let not the wife depart from her husband: But if she depart, let her remain unmarried, or be reconciled to her husband: and let not the husband put away his wife." (I Cor. 7:10,11).

Surely in the face of such fulness of evidence just presented, any honest and unbiased mind should have little difficulty in comprehending and accepting the fact that the two passages in Matthew which allow divorce and re-marriage were meant only for Jewish men under the law, and were never intended to apply to Christians.

CHAPTER SEVEN

CONTENTS

Separation, Divorce, Remarriage and Church Doctrine

Separation, Divorce, Remarriage, and Church Doctrine

As churches among the Gentiles multiplied in apostolic days it seems their difficulties increased. Notably true was this in the Church at Corinth in regard to marital matters. The Gentiles whose thoughts would be colored by Greek philosophy would want to settle these matters by their particular system of teaching. The Jewish believers who would be under the influence of Judaistic teachers would refer to the law of Moses and their national customs as their rule. Who was right in the controversy? Both were wrong. Finally an appeal is made to Paul the apostle in the form of written questions. The substance of these questions and Paul's answers to them are found in the seventh chapter of the first epistle to the Corinthians. These questions deal with such marital matters as: (1) marriage and celebacy—and the answer is given in (vv. 1-9); (2) separation, divorce and remarriage, and the answer is given in (vv. 10-17); (3) marriage and Christian service and the answer is found in (vv. 25-38); (4) marriage in the Lord and the answer given is found in vv. 39,40).

THE MARITAL PROBLEM OF THE CHURCH AT CORINTH

I shall now state, as it appears to me, the marital problem as it existed in the church at Corinth at the time of Paul's writing.

It seems that there was an element in the Church which dissaproved of the unmarried state (celebacy.) This part was probably Jewish, for the Jews believed that every man and every woman should be married. Paul defends the unmarried state against those who thought it was wrong and unchristian and points out its advantages chiefly in relation to serving the Lord (vv. 25-38). But those (the Greek element) who extolled the unmarried state to the extent of dissaproving of marriage altogether needed to be corrected and this the apostle does (in verse 2) by plainly stating that the mating of one man to one woman is the normal state in marital relations and that such an association aids in preserving purity of life.

Then there was a class—married persons who had the idea that to cease practicing the conjugal rights of the marriage bed would advantage them in their spiritual life. The apostle advises and warns in regard to following such a course. In verse 5 he states it must be by mutual consent, for a limited time only and for spiritual reasons. He also warns of the moral danger in pursuing such an unnatural course as it gave Satan an opening to tempt them in their incontinency—lack of self-control in sexual desires.

Then there was another class—married persons who believed that the Christian standard necessitated a complete physical separation or divorcement of married persons. Paul offsets such an idea by stating the Lord's ruling in such a case, he says, ''Unto the married I command, yet not I, but the Lord, Let not the wife depart from her husband, but if she deaprt, let her remain unmarried, or be reconciled to her husband: and let not the husband put away his wife'' (vv. 10,11). This ruling which discourages separation and prohibits both divorce and remarriage was the one accepted by the early Christians as the Lord's mind for them. Paul ordained it as permanent divine legislation for all Churches. (See I Cor. 7:17 and 14:37).

Still there was another class—those saved subsequent to

their marriage and whose partners remained in unbelief. This class thought it was scripturally incumbent upon them to separate from their heathen unbelieving partners on the ground that their marriage was an unequal yoke, or that incompatability demanded it. In giving a solution to this marital difficulty the apostle states that although the Lord Jesus had given an authoritative decision in the case where both partners were Christians (vv. 10,11), yet He had left no explicit answer to the question where a mixed marriage was involved. Paul under inspiration gives one. His statement implies that becoming a Christian is no ground for divorce, nor is the unbelief and unchristian behaviour of a partner in marriage. The answer is summed up in the following words, "As the Lord hath called every one, so let him walk. And so I ordain in every Church" (v. 17). If on the other hand the unbelieving partner separated, the believer must acquiesce. To insist on a continuation of the married relation would only lead to strife and a discrediting of the gospel. Although such a position gives the believer freedom from marital obligations yet it does not dissolve the marriage union. In such a case Paul says nothing about the believer being free to remarry. He had just stated the Lord's command (vv. 10,11), which denied Christians who had separated the right to remarry and it is only natural that the same prohibition applies to a Christian married to an unbeliever. To say the believer who has been deserted has freedom to remarry is to contradict the explicit command of Christ. (vv. 10,11).

In the light of such a background—these statements of facts just made in describing the marital problem that existed in the Church at Corinth I will seek to give in a series of questions and answers God's mind for the believer on the matter of divorce and remarriage.

A careful reader of Scripture will observe that Paul's teaching on separation, divorce and remarriage is in two parts—one which applies to couples that are both believers (1 Cor. 7:10,11), and the other dealing with mixed marriages where one of the mates is an unbeliever (vv. 12-16). The first part is distinguished by the words, "And unto the married I command, yet not I, but the Lord" (v. 10); the second, by the words, "But to the rest (mixed marriages) speak I, not the Lord" (v. 12). That is, the Lord left a ruling on divorce where both partners were believers, but none in the case of a mixed marriage. But here by divine inspiration Paul gives one.

In order that these two distinct rulings may be clearly distinguished and more easily apprehended I shall deal with them under two separate headings—"Believing Couples" and "Mixed Marriages." The latter to be taken up in Chapter eight.

Part One

FOR BELIEVING COUPLES

Question 1. Is it Scriptural for a Believing Wife to Divorce her Believing Husband and Remarry?

This question is answered by the commandment of the Lord, "Unto the married I command, yet not I, but the Lord. Let not the wife depart from her husband, but if she depart, let her remain unmarried" (Cor. 7:10,11).

How simple, yet how authoritative and uncompromising is the apostle's answer. The believing wife is bound by two prohibitions. One in regard to separation and the other to remarriage.

While the answer supposes that separation may take place, yet this must not be construed to mean that the Lord countenances such a thing or that the liberty to divorce is implied in it. Nor would resolving not to remarry justify the believing wife divorcing her husband.

The question may be asked, "Why is the prohibition regarding remarriage so uncompromising?" The answer would be that although separation and divorce are incompatible with true marriage, Christian blessings, beliefs, and conduct; remarriage is a more serious marital irregularity for it involves the forming of a relation which is termed an act of adultery. This ruling is plainly stated by the Lord Jesus in Mark 10:12, "And if a woman shall put away her husband, and be married to another she committeth adultery." How the apostle came to know this ruling is conjectural. That he did not get it by special revelation from the Lord he himself states. The most creditable answer is that he received it personally from the mouths of the apostles who accompanied the Lord.

Question II. Is a Believing Husband Permitted to DIVORCE HIS WIFE?

Again we shall let the word of the Lord answer, "Let not the husband put away his wife" (I Cor. 7:11). Man may add ifs, buts, and qualifications to this prohibition, but to the believer who desires to do the will of God and please the Lord, these few simple, yet weighty words settle the question of whether it is right or wrong for him to divorce his wife.

We would call the reader's attention to the fact that in answering the two foregoing questions the apostle did not reveal new teaching nor state a totally unknown ruling. His words, ''I command, yet not I, but the Lord,'' in effect amount to saying, ''The Lord has taught on the matter and His teaching is the fixed rule for the Christian.''

Nor is it something to be overlooked, or of minor importance that the substance of this ruling is the Lord's teaching on divorce and remarriage found in Mark 10:6-12—teaching that makes no allowance for divorce and which constitutes remarriage by a divorced person adultery. Why did Paul not base his teaching on the Lord's words of Matthew 5:32 and 19:9, verses wherein it is plainly stated that a husband was at liberty to put away his wife for the cause of fornication? Are we to assume he was ignorant of what Christ said in these passages? Or shall we attribute it to divine design on the part of the Holy Spirit of God? We believe the omission is divinely purposed and is another strong link of evidence as proof that these two utterances in Matthew are nothing more than a restatement and true interpretation of the Mosaic statute of divorce still applicable at the time the Lord spoke them to men under the law.

It will be readily granted that the Apostle Paul, in his care for and dealings with the churches, must have had many occasions for making use of the teaching found in Matthew 5:32 and 19:9 if these verses mean what so many Christian teachers today impute to them, namely, that a Christian has the right to divorce and remarry on the ground of adultery. Yet, never once are they so used, nor referred to in the epistles.

There is a rule that accredited interpreters of the scriptures follow in their exegesis of God's Word, I refer to the law of never using a doubtful passage to contradict a clear positive one. Let the reader put the following

94

words, "Unto the married I command, yet not I, but the Lord. Let not the wife depart from her husband, but if she depart, let her remain unmarried; and let not the husband put away his wife," (I Cor. 7:10,11), over against the words of Matthew 19:9 and he will find the one is at variance with the other. The Matthew passage permits divorce whereas the Corinthian one prohibits it. Such variations in doctrine are common in scripture and easily explained on the ground that each of these teachings belongs to a different dispensation—the Matthew passage to that of the law while the letter to the Church at Corinth belongs to the Christian dispensation.

THE RULE OF LAST MENTION

I call attention to another important fact, namely, that the words, "And let not the husband put away his wife" (I Cor. 7:11), are the last words in the progressive revelation of the truth of divorce. Now this is significant for the last part of the revelation of a truth always supersedes in its application the former parts which belong to and have their application in another dispensation.

(The truth of this assertion may be seen in regard to eating of meats. Before the flood there is no mention of the Creator sanctioning the eating of flesh. When a fresh start is made with Noah and his family we find God saying, "Every moving thing that liveth shall be meat for you; even as the green herb have I given you all things" (Genesis 9:3). When the Israelites are divinely formed into a nation the Lord prescribes that there are certain meats they should not eat. (See the whole of Leviticus chapter eleven). When the Lord Jesus called his disciples out of the Jewish fold to become the nucleus of His then future Church he taught them that eating meats defiled

95

no one. (Matt. 15:10-20). When He formed His Church and legislated for it through the apostles He removed all restrictions that had been placed by Moses on eating of meats. (See Paul's instructions to the Christians Rom. 14:1-15; to Timothy in I Tim. 4:3-5; and Peter's vision in Acts 11:5-9).

What was omitted before the flood was added after it. What was fully allowed to Noah was limited as edible to Israel. For the Christian the Jewish restrictions are removed; all meats are clean and edible to him.)

The full progressive revelation of the truth of divorce is as follows: (1) Divorce was first legalized and circumscribed by Moses and permitted to the male sex only in Israel (Deut. 24:1,2), (2) The Lord Jesus allowed the privilege as originally prescribed to remain in force to men in Israel, (Matt. 5:32; 19:9); (3) The Lord when speaking on divorce privately to His disciples made no allowance for it, and branded as an adulterer the divorced person who remarries (Mark 10:11,12), and (4) sixty years after the legal, ceremonial and judicial enactments of the law of Moses had been absolutely abrogated for the Christian (Romans 7:3,4) Paul gives the Lord's commandment for the Churches on divorce which is as follows: "Unto the married I command, yet not I, but the Lord, Let not the wife depart from her husband: But if she depart let her remain unmarried, or be reconciled to her husband: and let not the husband put away his wife" (1 Cor. 7:10,11).

The reader should have no difficulty in perceiving that the teaching of Moses on divorce is a variance with the Lord's teaching to His disciples and the Church. Though they vary yet they do not contradict one another. They are simply truth on divorce that belongs to two different

96

dispensations. Deuteronomy 24:1,2; Matthew 5:32; 19:9 being for the Jew under the law and Mark 10:11,12; Luke 16:18; 1 Cor. 7:10,11 being for the Lord's people in the present dispensation.

When the *Rule of Last Mention* is applied in appropriating God's mind on marital separation, divorce, and remarriage of divorced persons for His people today, whether they be a "Believing Couple" or a "Mixed Marriage" I unhesitatingly say it is found in First Corinthians 7:10-17.

CHAPTER EIGHT

CONTENTS

Separation, Desertion, Remarriage and Church Doctrine

CHAPTER EIGHT

Separation, Desertion, Remarriage and Church Doctrine

We will now take up the case of the person who was married prior to his conversion and whose partner remains in unbelief—in short a mixed marriage. *1 Cor.*

Part Two

MIXED MARRIAGES
QUESTION I: SHOULD CHRISTIANS LEAVE THEIR MARRIED PARTNERS BECAUSE THEY ARE UNBELIEVERS?

The apostle gives this answer: "If a brother hath a wife that believeth not, and she be pleased to dwell with him, let him not put her away. And the woman that hath a husband that believeth not and he be pleased to dwell with her, let her not leave him" (1 Cor. 7:11,12). How unmistakable is the answer. As long as the unbelieving mate is willing to live with the believer, God does not require nor is there any need for marital separation because of the fact that their marriage is an unequal yoke and has become uncongenial.

Old Testament Example

The book of Ezra records that many Jews which came back from the Babylonian captivity married heathen wives and thereby contracted ceremonial defilement. But in chapter 10, verses 1-4, we find them confessing their sin and taking measures according to the law to cleanse themselves from the polluted relationship by putting away the strange wives.

Now the Jewish believers in the church at Corinth whose minds were indoctrinated in the ceremonies of the Mosaic law, evidently had scruples about remaining in the marriage relation with one who was an unbeliever. They may have reasoned it was illegal and defiling and perhaps cited the action of the Jews in Ezra's days to prove that the Christian had a similar right and was obligated to separate from the unbelieving partner.

An Unchanging Principle

In meeting this argument the apostle states in a new way, an old and permanent principle inherent in marriage as constituted in the beginning which justifies a believer remaining in wedlock with an unbeliever. The principle I refer to is the unity made in marriage. (See Genesis 2:24; Matthew 19:6; Ephesians 5:31). This unity remains intact despite the fact the believer's married partner remains in unbelief and may live in wickedness. Death, not conduct, is that which dissolves the marriage bond. Indeed, it is the intrinsic oneness in marriage that is here said to take the unbelieving partner of heathen ground, that is the meaning of Paul's words, "For the unbelieving husband is sanctified (set apart) in the wife and the unbelieving wife is sanctified (set apart) in the husband" (1 Cor. 7:14, R. V.) The unbeliever obtains relative sanctification through the marriage union, without the impartation of any inherent holiness.

Futhermore, the apostle clearly implies that God sanctions and sanctifies the marriage made by believers in their unconverted days and expects that they will continue to faithfully discharge their marital responsibilities. Ignorance of what scripture teaches on this matter has led some believers to adopt a "holier than thou" attitude towards

100

their unbelieving mates and to withhold the conjugal rights and neglect their marital obligations. Such unwise, unnatural, and unscriptural conduct cannot be justified as proper on the plea that one must be faithful in the responsibility of serving the Lord. For God does not expect, far less require, a service that will result in the believer being negligent, unfaithful, or disobedient to any other responsibility. It is this attitude coupled with failure to fulfill their social, and domestic responsibilities that is the chief cause of so much marital unhappiness, disruption, and divorce connected with mixed marriages. And sad but true, even marriages where both partners are believers.

QUESTION II: SUPPOSE A BELIEVING WIFE* IS WILLING TO REMAIN WITH HER HUSBAND YET HE IS NOT WILLING TO REMAIN WITH HER AND MAY EVEN DIVORCE HER? (1) IN SUCH A CASE WHAT ACTION SHOULD SHE TAKE? (2) IS SHE FREE TO REMARRY?

THE ACTION SHE SHOULD TAKE

The words, "If the unbelieving depart let him depart" (1 Cor. 7:15), indicate that a Christian woman should not take any action at law to keep him under her roof nor to hold him to his marital obligations. Nor should she be a party to his obtaining a divorce, for to do so would make her a partaker in his breach of the marital covenant (Mal. 2:15). Furthermore, in consenting to a divorce, she would be partly responsible for his future course in marital and social disorder.

Moreover, the words, "For what knowest thou O wife, whether thou shalt save thy husband?" (16) clearly infer

---

* The same would apply to a believing husband.

that nothing more than physical separation is involved in her marital disruption; for although the unbelieving husband has departed she has still to regard him as her husband and seek his salvation. He may return and be reconciled but allowing a divorce would make this very improbable.

When one considers the exercise a believing wife should have for her unconverted husband who has deserted her, how can anyone teach that it is scriptural for a believing wife to divorce her unbelieving husband? Are these two things compatible—seeking his salvation and divorcing him?

IS SHE FREE TO REMARRY?

With regard to a believing wife whose husband has committed adultery against her having freedom to remarry, we feel sure that when the Scriptures are rightly divided and correctly interpreted it will be found she has no such liberty. Those who believe she (the so-called innocent party) has scriptural authority for divorcing ordinarily base their claim on Matthew 5:32 and 19:9— verses that without a doubt permit divorce and remarriage for the cause of fornication. But, before such a claim— "divorce on the ground of adultery" can be recognized as scripturally valid, the three following considerations ought to have our sober judgment. (1) Proof should be given that these two verses in Matthew are applicable to the Christian. We have already shown that they are not, but on the contrary apply exclusively to men under the law (chapter 6 of this book); (2) Proof should be given that the term "fornication" means "adultery." The reader is asked to consider our treatment of these two terms in chapter 5; and (3) Proof should be given that adultery dissolves the marriage union.

102

DOES ADULTERY DISSOLVE THE MARRIAGE UNION?

It appears to be universally accepted that adultery breaks the marriage bond. The veracity of this assertion has been little questioned and has gone unchallenged down through the ages. The world's judiciary having given such a ruling on adultery may be the chief contributing factor in its general acceptance. But we have looked in vain for one scripture from those who teach it in substantiation of it. It is simply a theory that is tacitly believed and accepted without question, despite the fact that it lacks scriptural warrant to support it. And it is generally the case that those who hold this line of doctrine also speak of marriage as being indissoluble. It would almost lead one to feel that our English language no longer has any fixed meaning, for if a thing be indissoluble how can adultery dissolve it.

A MISTRANSLATED SCRIPTURE

There is a passage of scripture in the book of Ezekiel, which as it appears in the Authorized Version would seem to indicate that marriage may be dissolved by some other cause than death. The passage I refer to is verse 38 of chapter 16 which reads as follows: "And I will judge thee, as women that break wedlock and shed blood are judged." Some have adduced from these words that adultery dissolves the marriage union. But the expression, "women that break wedlock" is the translator's interpretation instead of a literal translation of the Hebrew text. The translators were no doubt influenced in their thinking by the universal and common assumption that adultery breaks the marriage bond. The phrase, "women that break

103

wedlock" is in this place an interpretation of one Hebrew word *na'aph*. It is found over thirty times in the Old Testament and in every other case the term "adultery" is used for it. The Ezekiel passage is an unwarranted and misleading exception on the part of those who were responsible for the Authorized Version translation. The New Translation (J.N.D.) gives the proper rendering in the words, "women that commit adultery" rather than "women that break wedlock."

A MISAPPROPRIATED TEXT

"What? know ye not that he which is joined to an harlot is one body? for two saith he, shall be one flesh" (1 Cor. 6:16). These words have been made to mean that when a man commits adultery his marriage union no longer exists on the ground that another union has been formed. There is nothing in the context to indicate the apostle has married persons in mind or the dissolving of the marriage bond. On the other hand there is much to indicate that he is rebuking unmarried men who looked upon illicit sexual intercourse simply as an act of self gratification that involved no one else but themselves. The apostle dispels this ignorance and states the seriousness of such an act, by stating a principle drawn from the original constitution of marriage (v. 16). The Christian who commits fornication involves the Lord in the act for his body is a member of Christ. This inference may be taken from the words, "shall I then take the members of Christ and make them the members of an harlot" (v. 15). On the same principle the adulterer through his marriage union involves his married partner in his act.

Further proof that the apostle has unmarried persons in mind may be adduced from verse 18 of chapter 6,

104

and verse 2 of chapter 7. In these verses he gives a prevention against and a cure for fornication. The preventive is in fleeing from it, and having no confidence in the flesh. In a similar connection the apostle warns against self confidence, "Wherefore let him that thinketh he standeth take heed lest he fall" (1 Cor. 10:12). The cure is given in the following words, "Nevertheless to avoid fornication, let every man have his own wife, and let every woman have her own husband." Such advice would not apply to a person already married.

THE EFFECTS OF ADULTERY

The scriptural idea of adultery, as to its nature, relation, and the extent of its disorderly effects, is: (1) Sexual unfaithfulness to a married partner (Ezek. 16:32,) (2) the breaking of a covenant (Prov. 2:17), (3) the defiling of the marriage bed, (1 Chron. 5:1; Heb. 13:4), (4) a reproach that is never wiped away (Prov. 6:32,33), and (5) under the law without exception was punishable by death (Lev. 20:10), where adequate witness established guilt.

If we accept the idea that adultery dissolves the marriage union, then it necessarily follows that Abraham was no longer married to Sarah after having had illicit relations with Hagar. It further follows that the believer who continues to live with his wife who has committed adultery against him, and whom he has forgiven, does so in an unmarried relation. We would then be placed in a position where we would be forced to admit that where adultery has taken place the marriage union no longer exists. If such be the case, then there are tens of thousands of persons unmarried who do not know it. Would we be prepared to assent to such a thing?

Our assertion that adultery does not dissolve the marriage union is based on the inherent oneness that is formed in marriage in the beginning. This was confirmed by the Lord Jesus (Mark 10:6-9), and taught by Paul the apostle (Ephes. 5:31). Nor is the confirmation of the indissolubility of the marriage union confined to the teaching of the Lord Jesus and Paul the apostle. The same is done by the prophet Malachi. In his prophesy (chapter 2.) he shows that notwithstanding many Jews had divorced their wives and married others, that the original marriage tie was not dissolved. To those involved in this marital disorder which is plain open adultery, the prophet in effect says, notwithstanding you have divorced your wives *"yet* (emphasis on yet) she is thy companion, the wife of thy covenant." These words spoken four thousand years after marriage was constituted clearly prove that the mind of God regarding it was not affected by time, nor by a change in dispensation. Also, the union formed in it is not dissolved by such circumstance as adultery, polygamy or re-marriage.

Some have reasoned that making adultery a capital offense under the law was God's way of indicating the marriage union was dissolved by such sin. But this is false reasoning for the simple reason that many other crimes, some with lesser degrees of guilt and some with a greater degree, were punished with death under the law.

INDISSOLUBILITY TAUGHT IN FIGURE

The relation that existed between the nation of Israel and Jehovah may also be used to prove that adultery, desertion, or divorce do not dissolve the marriage tie. Although Israel, the spouse of Jehovah, had committed spiritual adultery against Him by their illicit intercourse

106

with the Gentiles, and notwithstanding they had deserted Him, yet their relation to Him as wife remained. In Jeremiah 3:1,14, the Lord says, "They say, if a man put away his wife, and she go from him, and become another man's, shall he return unto her again. Shall not the land be greatly polluted? But thou has played the harlot with many lovers; yet return unto me saith the Lord. Turn, O blacksliding children saith the Lord; for I am married unto you." Some day a reconciliation between Israel and Jehovah will take place. They have been put away but not *cast away*. (Isa. 50:1; 54:5-8; Jer. 3:1-18; Ezek. 16:1-63; Hosea 1:11; 2:1-23; 3:1-5).

The same thing is taught in figure by Paul in Ephesians where he uses marriage to set forth the union that exists between Christ and His body the Church. He writes, "For this cause shall a man leave father and mother and shall be joined unto his wife, and the twain shall be one flesh. This is a great mystery but I speak concerning Christ and the Church" (5:30-32). It will be readily admitted that no demerit on the part of one who is a member of Christ's body could effect a dissolution of the unity that makes him one spirit with the Lord (1 Cor. 6:17). Is it then divine wisdom for the apostle to use the marriage relation to portray the Church's union with Christ if the bond formed in marriage could be dissolved by the act of adultery?

DESERTION NOT GROUNDS FOR REMARRIAGE

There are others who in their extremity go so far as to make desertion ground for divorce and remarriage. Their authority for this is one lone verse found in chapter 7 of the First Epistle to the Corinthians, "If the unbelieving depart let him depart, a brother or a sister is not in bondage in such cases" (v. 15). When this passage is interpreted in the light of its context it will be seen that the writer is not dealing with remarriage of believers, but rather with their social and civil status in view of being deserted. The words simply mean that should this happen, the Christian is not under any divine or civil law which obligates him to remain enslaved to the departed unbeliever. In other words, if the unbelieving partner is determined to separate, the believer should not think it incumbent on him to forcibly prevent it. The believer is called in peace and nothing should be done to disturb it. The act of desertion, however, released from all marital responsibilities without dissolving the marriage tie.

MEANING OF THE WORDS "NOT UNDER BONDAGE"

They who contend for liberty to remarry on the ground of desertion, lay particular stress on the words, "is not under bondage."

When the word "bondage" (not bond) in the passage we are considering is interpreted by the Holy Spirit's use of it in other parts of Scripture it will be seen that it has nothing to do with the bond formed by marriage. The Greek word *duoloo,* translated *"bondage"* means *"to enslave."* It occurs only eight times in the New Testament and is translated four times *"bondage"* three times *"servant"* and once *"given."* We find it first in Acts 7:15 where it is used in connection with the nation of Israel being in *"bondage"* in Egypt; secondly, in II Peter 2:19, where it refers to persons being in *"bondage"* to sin; thirdly, in Romans 6:18,22 where it denotes the state of the believer, who was once in bondage to sin but is now the "servant"—*(duoloo)* of righteousness and of God; fourthly, in Titus where it is used to describe the godly behavior which becometh aged women. They should not be "*given*"—*(duoloo)* enslaved to much wine.

MEANING OF THE WORD "BOUND"

In contradistinction the Greek word used to denote the bond one is brought into by marriage is *deoo* which literally means "*to be bound by tieing a knot.*" It is used by the Apostle Paul three times when making mention of the marriage union. (See Romans 7:2; 1 Corinthians 7:27,39). Surely the apostle's use of these two words *duoloo* and *deoo* (closely related etymologically and socially) is conclusive proof that the freedom the deserted believer has, spoken of in 1 Corinthians 7:15 does not imply liberty to remarry. There is a rule that accredited interpreters of Scripture follow in their exegesis of it. I refer to the law of never using a doubtful or obscure passage to contradict a clear and positive one. When this law is applied to the interpretation of 1 Corinthians 7:15, it will be found that to make it mean that a believer who has been deserted has freedom to remarry is to contradict the plain words of Scripture.

The difference in the result of properly and improperly apprehending the truth of the text we are considering is so serious in its moral, ecclesiastical and social consequences that I deem it wise and beneficial to use the written ministry of a very learned and spiritually minded man as a testimony to the truth of the assertion I have just made.

Writing on this passage he says, "Thus, if the unbelieving party in the relationship were to sever himself from the other, the believer is released from bondage, be

109

it brother or sister in the case. Not that such an act on the unbeliever's side gives to the believer thus abandoned license to *remarry*, but that the believer is left the more free to serve the Lord by the other's separation. Such a union after all is apt to involve strife, the natural man hating the life of the Spirit. Not that this would involve anything on the believer's part to break the marriage tie: the unbeliever is supposed to have broken it himself or even herself; and "in peace hath God called us" (or you) not to seek separation. On the contrary, whatever the trial involved in such a life, the brother or the sister must earnestly desire the salvation of the unbeliever; but this is after all in God's disposal. "For what knowest thou, woman, if thou shalt save the husband?, or what knowest thou, husband, if thou shalt save the wife?" If it were so, what a joy! We have to acquiesce therefore in the ordering of the Lord and as we should on no account take the inititative into our own hands, so also to save the unbeliever is a question, and should not swamp everything else. Thus the apostle here cautions by pressing the rule, whatever the issue: "Only as the Lord divided to each, as God called each, so let him walk." This was intended to guard against undue or excessive feeling. Our place is one of intelligent subjection owning the Lord's allotment and God's call: the one at the time of conversion, the other the permanent condition. So ought each to walk." (William Kelly in his exposition of 1 Corinthians).

To the above quotation I would add an extract from the scholarly and spiritual work—the Numercial Bible by F. W. Grant. "But, on the other hand, if, on the side of the unbeliever, he departed, then, in such cases, the brother or the sister, says, the apostle is not bound. He or she is not obliged to recognize anymore the relationship as existing.

Yet the apostle does not mean by this, anything equivalent to *divorce,* or that which would *set absolutely free* the one separated from.''

Furthermore, when the words, ''a brother or a sister is not in bondage in such cases'' is interpreted by the rule of accumulative evidence there is such a preponderous weight of proof against making them mean that the abandoned believer has liberty to remarry that it is difficult to understand how anyone acquainted with such evidence can do so.

The evidence I refer to is (1) the Lord's words in Mark 10:11,12; Luke 16:18; (2) The Lord's command quoted by Paul, ''Let not the wife leave her husband, but if she depart let her remain *unmarried* . . . and let not the husband put away his wife'' (1 Cor. 7:10,11); (3) What Paul wrote further on in the same chapter ''The wife is bound by the law as long as her husband liveth; but if her husband be dead, she is at liberty to be married to whom she will only in the Lord''; and, (4) The plain, positive and unqualified statement of Romans 7:2,3, which brands a woman an adulteress who remarries while her husband is still alive.

I would ask the proponents of remarriage on the ground of desertion a condemning question. How do you reconcile teaching that a Christian has the right to use Matthew 5:32 and 19:9, Scriptures that confine divorce and remarriage to one exception—fornication—with believing that desertion is also a cause for remarriage?

I will now state ten reasons as proof that it is unscriptural for a Christian to divorce and remarry.

111

TEN REASONS WHY A CHRISTIAN SHOULD NOT DIVORCE AND REMARRY

The *first* of these reasons is based on marriage as instituted in the beginning (Gen. 2:24). Divorce is not in its constitution. Nor would it be comtemplated seeing it was inaugurated in the state of innocency.

The *second* reason is based on the following three fold witness: Prophet Malachi, the Lord Jesus, and Paul the Apostle. Each of these restated and confirmed that marriage as originally ordained is still binding and does not permit polygamy, divorce or remarriage of divorced persons. (Mal. 2:14-16; Mark 10:3-9; Eph. 5:31).

The *third* is based on the fact that permission to put away a wife was given by Moses to men of the nation of Israel, and he never legislated for the Church. However the Lord allowed the Mosaic privilege of divorce to remain for men in Israel who had not become His disciples.

The *fourth*: Because of the obvious absence of any permission to divorce being granted by the Lord to His disciples or by the apostles to the church.

The *fifth* is drawn from the Lord's prohibition: "What therefore (not whom) God hath joined together, let not man put asunder" (Matt. 19:6), and His command, "Let not the husband put away his wife" and "if she depart let her remain unmarried or be reconciled to her husband" (1 Cor. 7:11).

The *sixth* is taken from the truth taught in the following apostolic injunction: "The wife hath not power of her own body, but the husband: and likewise also the husband hath not power of his own body, but the wife" (1 Cor. 7:4). Divorce supposes that either one of the parties in

112

marriage takes their body from under the authority of the other. The injunction prohibits such acting.

The *seventh* : Because Christians are told to love their wives in the manner and measure that Christ loves the Church. Is divorcing one's wife consistent with such an injunction and requirement? (Eph. 5:25).

The *eighth* : Because of the principle that is contained in the following words, "He that loveth his wife, loveth himself" (Eph. 5:28). Is divorcing one's wife consistent with loving one's self? Could a person divide himself?

The *ninth* : Because it is not consistent with the grace of God wherein a Christian stands. Christians are expected to be imitators of God in the matter of forgiveness (Eph. 4:32; 5:1). Although adultery is spoken of in Scripture as a heineous sin and a reproach that is never wiped away, yet it should not be looked upon as an unpardonable sin.

The *tenth* : Because Christians are prohibited from taking one another before the world's courts. (1 Cor. 6:1). The only way to obtain a legal divorce is by judiciary action.

113

CHAPTER NINE

CONTENTS

Divorce, Remarriage and Church Reception

Divorce and Church Reception

We will now consider the Church's* corporate responsibility towards divorced persons as it relates to receiving
such "in the Lord as becometh saints" (Romans 16:2).
The persons we have under consideration are those who
have been divorced after becoming Christians.

* I use the term "church" in its local sense which may
be defined as follows: "A local Church is an assembly of
professed believers on the Lord Jesus Christ, living for the
most part in one locality, who assemble themselves together
in (unto) His name for the breaking of bread, worship,
praise, prayer, testimony, the ministry of the Word, discipline, and the furtherance of the gospel (Heb. 10:25;
Acts 20:7; 11:26; 1 Cor. 5:4,5; 11:18,20; 14:26; Phil.
4:14-18; 1 Thess. 1:8; Acts 13:1-4). Such a Church exists
where two or three are thus gathered (Matt. 18:20). Every
such local church has Christ in its midst, is a temple of
God, and indwelt by the Holy Spirit (1 Cor. 3:16,17).
When perfected in organization a local church consists of
"saints, with the bishops (elders) and deacons."

RECEIVING INTO THE CHURCH

The subject and practice of receiving into the local
church has been and still is a matter of contention. It is
not the design of this paper to deal with the causes of this
contention, nor to treat with reception in general. We shall
confine ourselves to the subject as it affects divorced persons.

Just as there are divergent views found among Chris-

115

tians on the interpretation of the doctrine of divorce, even so there are differences among the churches as to what constitutes fitness on the part of a divorced person for receiving "the right hands of *fellowship*" (Gal. 2:9).

These differences in the main may be briefly stated as follows: Some churches mutually receive divorced persons providing they were divorced on the ground of adultery and have *not remarried*. Others will receive a divorced person who has been remarried providing the divorce was obtained on the ground of adultery. Then there are those who will not receive a person who while in the status of a Christian has married a divorced person.

A Christian's behaviour is the true criterion of how he has apprehended the truth and is governed by it. These dissimilarities are the consequence of practicing truth as it has been apprehended. A wrong doctrine can only produce a wrong practice. And truth wrongly divided is sure to create contention and confusion. Indeed the root cause for the differences that exist among Christians on divorce and remarriage are the two following aberrations in apprehending the truth, namely: (1) Matthew 5:32 and 19:9 are scriptures that have been wrongly divided, and (2) the term "fornication" has been misinterpreted by being made to mean adultery.

WHO SHOULD BE RECEIVED?

The class of persons we advocate for reception conforms in character, strictly to the doctrine found in Matthew 19:4-8; Mark 10:6-12; Luke 16:18 and 1 Corinthians 7:10,11. In substance these verses state three undeniable and irrefutable certainties: (1) The Lord Jesus confirmed that marriage as originally constituted is still applicable to the whole human family; (2) He gave no allowable

116

cause for divorce to His disciples; (3) He emphatically declared remarriage by illegally divorced persons, or marriage to such divorced persons to be adultery. On the basis of such plain teachings we shall give rulings in dealing with "who should be received." This we propose to do in a series of questions. It should thoroughly be understood that only persons who have been divorced after becoming Christians are contemplated in the questions. The case of those involved in divorcement before becoming Christians will be taken up in chapter ten.

QUESTION I: SHOULD THE CHURCH RECEIVE A CHRISTIAN WHO HAS DIVORCED HIS MARRIED PARTNER ON THE GROUND OF ADULTERY?

ANSWER: Whilst this action on the part of a Christian is clear disobedience to the teaching of the Scriptures (Matt. 19:6; 1 Cor. 7:10,11), yet it may have been done in ignorance of the Lord's command—"And unto the married I command, yet not I, but the Lord, let not the wife depart from her husband: But if she depart let her remain unmarried, or be reconciled to her husband: and let not the husband put away his wife" (1 Cor. 7:10,11). On the other hand it may have been the result of receiving misinformation, such as: (1) the belief that there is no difference in meaning between the terms fornication and adultery, and that both are used in an interchangeable way in the New Testament; or, (2) that Matthew 5:32 and 19:9 is teaching that applies to the Christian. While ignorance cannot be condoned nor the act of ignorantly misappropriating Scripture be justified; nevertheless, they ought to have some consideration.

To divorce one's partner on the ground of adultery,

117

may not be failure of such a nature that would debar one from fellowship. Nevertheless, the person who is guilty of it cannot be said to be blameless. As blamelessness in marital relations is a necessity in the character of those who hold office and serve in the church (1 Tim. 3:2,12; Titus 1:6,7), consequently such divorced persons should be received with the following restrictions: (1) they cannot hold office in the church or take public part in its services; and (2) their right to remain in church fellowship is contingent upon their abiding unmarried while their divorced partner is alive.

QUESTION II: SHOULD THE SAME TREATMENT APPLY TO THE SO-CALLED INNOCENT PARTY?

ANSWER: In the case of the innocent party, that is, where his conduct was not the cause for the divorce, nor did he take the initiative in obtaining it, a difference should be made. As no direct blame attaches to him in the disruption, the prohibitory restrictions regarding leadership and service in the church would not apply to him. Nevertheless, the necessity to remain unmarried would be binding and adherence to this rule while his divorced partner still lived would be one determining factor as to his fitness for remaining in fellowship.

QUESTION III: SHOULD THE CHURCH RECEIVE A CHRISTIAN WHO REMARRIES AFTER HAVING BEEN DIVORCED?*

ANSWER: Such a person is not scripturally eligible to be received. It is not the fact that he has been divorced that debars him. Divorce in itself only caused a disruption

---

* This does not refer to persons who were legally divorced prior to being converted.

118

in the married relation. But remarriage while his divorced partner is alive would bring him into an extra marital association which Scripture calls adulterous. This ruling is based on the Lord's teaching, "Whosoever shall put away his wife, and marrieth another committeth adultery against her. And if a woman shall put away her husband, and be *married* to another, she committeth adultery" (Mark 10:11,12; Luke 16:18). When these verses of Scripture are interpreted in the light of their circumstantial and contextual setting, it will be clearly seen that they definitely apply to the Christian. Furthermore, the fact that the teaching of these verses is at variance with that of Matthew 5:32 and 19:9 is sufficient and decisive evidence that the Matthew passages are to be practiced only under the dispensation of the law and are not applicable to the Christian.

Concerning God's house we read, "Holiness becometh thine house, O Lord, for ever" (Psalm 93:5). Would receiving a person living in a permanent adulterous relation be consistent with maintaining the holiness feature that should ever characterize God's house? To be debarred from the membership-fellowship and privileges of the church is the high price a Christian pays for the disobedient and self-gratifying act of remarrying while his (her) former partner is still alive.

QUESTION IV: SHOULD THE CHURCH RECEIVE A CHRISTIAN WHO MARRIES A DIVORCED PERSON?

ANSWER: Such a person should not be received.* This uncompromising ruling demands an explanation. It is

---

* This ruling would not apply in certain cases where the person they married was involved in divorcement prior to being saved.

based on the Lord's words, "Whosoever putteth away his wife and marrieth another committeth adultery: and *whosoever marrieth her that is put away committeth adultery*" (Luke 16:18). It is difficult to make these words mean any other thing than that the Christian who marries a divorced person is brought under the same guilty status and is classified as being partaker with such in marital disorder, which is plainly said to be adultery.

A WARNING

Some churches (so called) who are either not governed by Scripture, or who have no respect for the holiness of God's house, totally ignore the question of divorce and remarriage in their mutual reception of Christians.

Then there are churches who put a difference between the innocent and the guilty parties. They will receive only the innocent party who is remarried providing the divorce was abtained on the ground of adultery.

However, there are churches whose practice in reception is based on the words of the Lord Jesus, rightly divided, correctly interpreted, and properly appropriated. Consequently, they will not receive any person who, after having become a Christian, is divorced and then remarried while his former partner still is alive; nor will they receive a person who has married a divorced Christian if that divorced person's partner is still living.

One can readily see how the carelessness, indifference, and imperfect practice of the first two instances cited may produce a problem when persons from these churches present themselves for reception. It further adds to the difficulty, when such persons come commended by letter, for it seems to be an unwritten law that such a thing should be looked upon as a ticket of admission, or a passport which carries with it the privilege of granting the bearers immunity from examination when determining their fitness for church fellowship. Rather should a letter be viewed as a condensed biography of the person commended and as a church safeguard.

ADVICE

In view of the prevalence of divorce among professing Christians and the loose views many hold on the matter, we would exhort those who have the chief responsibility of receiving to be continually exercised and vigilant concerning this evil which in the light of Scripture is truly a moral menace to the local church testimony. Futhermore, we would advise that all applicants for permanent fellowship-membership (whether vouched for by persons or commended by letter) be examined orally on the matter of their marital relations as a safeguard in maintaining discipline and the holiness feature of God's house. (Psalm 93:5; 1 Cor. 3:17).

CHAPTER TEN

CONTENTS

Divorce, Remarriage and Church Fellowship

CHAPTER TEN

Divorce, Remarriage and Church Fellowship

The matter which we shall now consider concerns Christians who before their conversion were involved in marital disorder. The question as to whether these persons should be or should not be admitted into the local church fellowship is what we would seek to answer. The importance of producing, fostering, and maintaining harmonious relations among brethren in the Lord calls for some prefatory remarks. I believe these will throw some light and help to remove the differences of opinion that exist among Christians on the matter.

PREFATORY REMARKS

The Spirit of God has given a brief yet full delineation of the moral, social, and religious conditions which would characterize Christendom in the last days of the church's history on the earth. (See II Timothy 3:1-13). When this prophetic foreview is compared with the description in Romans 1:28-31 of the heathen world it will be seen that the two correspond the one to the other. Today we see a strange anomaly—heathenism taking on the outward features of Christianity and Christendom fast returning to a state descriptive of heathenism.

One menacing social evil which is slowly emerging and showing its ugly head in every part of Christendom is the abnormality of divorce in marriage. This marital impropriety is in essence the fruit of unbridled lust (II Chronicles 11:23; Luke 17:27). It would be prevalent in every Protestant and Catholic country were it not for their laws that curb and prevent it.

123

This assertion is borne out by what happened in Russia following the First World War. When the Bolsheviks came to power, one of their outstanding social experiments was the inauguration of a system under which divorce could be had for the asking, and without delay, by either party in the marriage. In one suburb of Moscow alone, for one year, there were 2,906 divorces as against 3,862 marriages. Gradually in the whole country divorces and remarriages increased until they reached an astronomical figure. This was having such a demoralizing and disorganizing effect on the nation's social life that the government was forced to amend its divorce law in order to preserve its society from complete disintegration.

Today in the United States of America there exists a condition similar to that of Russia almost three decades ago. It probably is no exaggeration to say, that there are more divorces granted in the United States each year than in all the countries of Christendom put together during the same period of time. The latest census shows that for the 1,811,155 marriages contracted in 1948 there were 408,000 divorces during the same period.* In the same year the state of California had 42,800 divorces over against 88,242 marriages.* In the country as a whole, there are thousands of people who are known to have been divorced and remarried many times over.

A CHURCH PROBLEM

Scripture shows and experience proves that churches very much reflect the natural characteristics of their members, and that their problems are largely created by the con-

* In 1946 there were 2,291,045 marriages and 610,000 divorces.
* In 1949 Nevada led the nation in the number of divorces. It had 10,800 divorces—an average of 6.9 for every 1000 persons of its population.

ditions that prevail in the communities in which they are set.

Some of the epistles of the New Testament written to churches resident in the cities of different countries reveal this. The Church at Corinth and the Church at Philippi are examples of this very thing. The First Epistle to the Corinthians makes manifest the social, religious and immoral character of the city of Corinth, as well as revealing the sophistical and priggish type of mind that characterized the Grecian people. In contrast to this, the high moral standard of the city of Philippi, the magnanimous soul, the cheerful spirit, the lowly mind and peace loving disposition of the Macedonian people are clearly made visible in the epistle to the Philippians.

The history of modern missions in heathen lands reveals that heathen ideas and practices connected with marriage created a problem in the founding and forming of *local* churches and in their subsequent care.

No longer is this marital problem confined to heathen lands. The loose ideas that many in Christendom hold on marriage, together with the prevalence of divorce, constitutes a new exercise to the churches in Protestant countries. The chief contributer to this issue is the United States of America.

This marital menace, because of its ramifications and widespread effects combined with the ease of travel, is bound in time to adversely affect churches all over the English speaking world. It is even now presenting a difficulty to churches in America. Being a comparatively new problem many of these are at a loss as to how it should be handled.

It is quite obvious that the problem is connected with the social condition of the nation. Every year hundreds of thousands of persons are divorced. Each year tens of thousands of persons profess conversion to Christ. By natural process it is to be expected that at least a small percentage of these will have been involved in the divorce evil prior to their conversion. Becoming a Christian and joining a church seem to be natural accompaniments. It is the joining part that creates an exercise for the churches. We will now consider the subject in detail.

QUESTION: SHOULD PERSONS WHO HAVE BEEN DIVORCED AND REMARRIED PRIOR TO THEIR CONVERSION BE ADMITTED INTO THE LOCAL CHURCH FELLOWSHIP?

ANSWER: IF A PERSON'S DIVORCE AND REMARRIAGE IS LEGAL ACCORDING TO THE RULE OF HUMAN GOVERNMENT HE SHOULD BE ADMITTED, PROVIDING HE IS ABLE TO MEET THE OTHER SCRIPTURAL REQUIREMENTS.

FIVE REASONS FOR ADMITTING THEM

The first reason I would give for receiving the persons under consideration is based on the silence of the Word of God regarding it. We know of no direct scripture statement that says they should be or that they should not be received. Surely there is a divine design in this silence as there is in every matter on which Scripture has nothing to say. Anyone acquainted with the moral and social conditions that prevailed in apostolic days does not for a moment doubt that some who believed the gospel had in their lives before conversion irregularities from the first form of marriage. Furthermore, not only is scripture specifically silent on receiving the class of persons we are considering, but there is also no record of the matter

126

being a problem or a cause of contention in the primitive churches. Surely there was much more cause in the apostolic era for it being a church difficulty than today. I believe we are warranted in deducing from this twofold silence the inference that such persons were received into the membership-fellowship of the Church. One would not seek to be wiser than Scripture by stating supposed reasons for this silence.

SECOND REASON

The second reason for receiving is based on the following: According to (Luke 24:47; Acts 10:43; 13:39; 2 Cor. 5:17), a person upon repentance and belief on the Lord Jesus Christ receives forgiveness of sins, he is justified from all guilt and he has become a new creation in Christ. The sin incurred in remarriage is but one of the many sins from which he is justified. If his fitness for fellowship be contingent upon his behavior before conversion then it naturally follows that the apostle Paul should have been debarred from the fellowship of the saints on the ground that he was implicated in persecuting unto death many of the saints prior to his conversion (Acts 22:20; 26:1-10.) Furthermore, by such a standard of reception neither could the woman of Sychar's well have been received because she had had five husbands and was at the time of her conversion living in an unmarried association with a sixth man (John 4:16-18.) Had she been married to this man, it is quite clear from the tenor of scripture, the Lord would not have said, "He whom thou hast is not thy husband." My reason for mentioning this is, some have supposed that the woman was married to the man and notwithstanding this the Lord did not recognize the marriage relation as existing. Nevertheless, to qualify for reception

127

she would have to cease living in the unlawful and unscriptural marital association found in at the time of her conversion.

Since the above was written there has appeared in a monthly magazine having an international circulation and known for its soundness of teaching, the following item:

QUESTION: "A woman brought to Christ through the instrumentality of a young man in her employment has been converted and baptised and now wishes assembly fellowship. She has twice been divorced and is now married for the third time—all this transpired before she was saved. As she cannot return to her first husband (he is legally married again,—can she be denied assembly fellowship?

ANSWER: Difficult situations sometimes present themselves, and like Paul we ask—"Who is sufficient for these things?" Surely "our sufficiency is of God." Since He has justified the sinner and made her to taste of the fulness of Divine grace; making her a "new creation" in Christ Jesus (2 Cor. 5:17): What else could be done with such an one, but to receive her as Christ already has done to the glory of God.

There are things which may be adjusted in the afterlife of a person who believes; e.g., *debt* or *theft*—such should be repaid or returned so that the conscience may be clear. A case like this one, however, would be difficult to adjugate in if it were insisted that the acts prior to conversion must be adjusted. It would be much easier and involve less to accept the person as she was found when converted. In the case of a heathen who may have had many marriages and whose life was very questionable before the grace of God reached him and transformed him, one could but accept him as he was found upon conversion.

128

THIRD REASON

The third reason is based on the Apostle Paul's description of the kind of character some in the Church at Corinth had before being converted. In enumerating some of the practicers of evil who will not inherit the kingdom of God, he mentions "adulterers" and "fornicators" and then follows his words to the Church, "and such were some of you, but ye are washed, but ye are sanctified (set apart) but ye are justified (cleared from all guilt) in the name of the Lord Jesus and by the Spirit of our God" (1 Cor. 6:9,11). It is quite obvious that many who had once been a part of the moral scum of the city of Corinth, had been converted to the Lord Jesus and were a recognized part of the community of saints—the local church, scripturally termed "the fellowship of our Lord Jesus Christ" (1 Cor. 1:9).

FOURTH REASON

The fourth reason I would give for receiving this class of believers without requiring them to disrupt the humanly legalized marriage in which they may be found in at the time of their conversion is based on 1 Cor. 7:12,13,17, "If any brother hath a wife that believeth not, and she be pleased to dwell with him, let him not put her away? . . . And the woman which hath a husband that believeth not and if he be pleased to dwell with her, let her not leave him." . . . "But as God hath distributed to every man, as the Lord hath called everyone, so let him walk: And so ordain I in all the churches" (1 Cor. 7:12,13,17). When these words are viewed in the light of the fact that they are an answer to questions regarding the advisability or necessity of disturbing the married relationship the believer is found in at the time of his conversion, there is ample justification for deducing from them the inference that a Christian should continue to live in the conjugal state he is found in at conversion. The married relationship, however, should be a legal one in the eyes of the civil authorities (Romans 13:2-6; 1 Peter 2:13,14), and should not come under the condemnation of Scripture.

FIFTH REASON

The fifth reason I would give for receiving persons who were divorced and remarried in what Scripture calls, *"the pastime of our life"* (1 Pet. 4:3) is deduced from 1 Timothy 3:2,12, "A bishop must be blameless, the husband of one wife." "Let the deacons (servants) be the husbands of one wife." The implication here is that there were in the church at Ephesus some who had more than one wife. But although such were not at that stage in the church's historical experience debarred from its fellowship, yet they were disqualified from ruling and publicly serving among the saints.*

This scripture in Timothy has such an important bearing on the question of receiving that I deem it helpful to use the words of a man of international reputation and recognized to be one of the ablest, sanest and unprejudiced expositors of Holy Scripture. Interpreting 1 Timothy 3:2, he writes, "Certain weighty qualifications, and circumstances morally clear were to be sought in such as desired to do this excellent work. Moral qualifications, not gifts, are requisite and personal or relative circumstances of good report. Hence, to be the husband of one wife was sought as well as a character free from reproach. Again if a man had more than one wife, he was (*NOT TO BE REFUSED FELLOWSHIP*: for many a Jew or Gentile

---

* See pages 32 and 33 for how the church should treat such persons today.

so situated might believe the gospel; but ineligible to be a holy guardian of order according to God among the saints" (William Kelly).

QUALIFICATIONS IN RECEIVING

Having covered the subject in a general way, we shall now consider specific cases involved in marital irregularities that have requirements that would have to be met by the persons involved before they could be received.

QUESTION I: SHOULD THE CHURCH ADMIT INTO ITS FELLOWSHIP A MAN WHO IS LIVING WITH A WOMAN (KNOWN AS A COMMON-LAW WIFE) AND A FAMILY HAS BEEN BORN TO THEM?

ANSWER: This man should not be admitted in the state in which "the Lord hath called" (1 Cor. 7:17) him, for the following reason: He is living in an illegal and unscriptural association. To qualify for fellowship he must: (1) disassociate himself from the immoral practice and rectify this irregular situation, for in the eyes of the world, as well as of God, he is a law breaker; and (2) he must obey the Scriptures which require that the human race be propagated in the married state as constituted by the creator in the beginning—one male and one female joined together and becoming one flesh. Thus he must officially marry the woman with whom he has been living in the unmarried state.

QUESTION II: SHOULD THE CHURCH ADMIT INTO ITS FELLOWSHIP A MAN WHO IS LIVING IN SEPARATION FROM HIS MARRIED PARTNER?

ANSWER: Before being received this person should be advised to seek a reconciliation with his separated partner. This would be in harmony with the original institution of marriage, the love and grace of God, and what is expected of one professing to be saved. But in the event of a refusal by the other party, the believer having met all necessary requirements to put right the wrong has nothing to hinder him from being received. However he should be made to understand that his eligibility to continue in church fellowship is contingent upon him not remarrying while his separated partner is still living in a state of separation.* In this case the Believer's predicament amounts to having been deserted. This kind of disruption is dealt with in 1 Corinthians 7:15. A reconciliation is still possible as long as the partner who deserted is still alive and not remarried.

Let the believer in this trial, wait upon God to sustain him and make the way of escape, both things He has promised to do. And let him take comfort and hope from God's promise to His children in such a trial, "For what knowest thou, O wife, whether thou shalt save thy husband? or how knowest thou, O man, whether thou shalt save thy wife?" (1 Cor. 7:16).

QUESTION III: SHOULD A MAN WHO IS THE HUSBAND OF AND IS LIVING WITH MORE THAN ONE WIFE BE ADMITTED INTO CHURCH FELLOWSHIP?

ANSWER: AS SUCH THIS PERSON SHOULD NOT BE RECEIVED.

This ruling is based on the teaching of the Lord Jesus and Paul the Apostle who both restated and confirmed the original institution of marriage—(one man and one woman becoming one flesh) always was and still remains God's

---

*It seems to me this prohibition would not apply in a case where the man's partner in the divorce had remarried while he was still in an unsaved state.

132

mind for His creature man (Mark 10:6-9; Eph. 5:31). Because the law of the land where a church is resident permits a man to have more than one wife, that does not warrant it being a legitimate practice for the Christian. While the Christian has to be subject to the *"powers that be"* (Rom. 13:1-6), and is also entitled to the privileges of the government he lives under; however when the enactments and the privileges of the civil authorities conflict with God's Word the course of the Christian is clear: The Word of God must have first claim on his obedience. (See Acts 5:29). This policy may entail suffering and the forfeiture of a privilege which is humanly legal; nevertheless it is the course that pleases God and characterizes Christianism.

While there is no open denunciation of polygamy in the New Testament, yet the divine standard of marriage is so clearly stated, restated and emphasized therein as to leave no one in doubt that polygamy is an irregularity in marriage and an unchristian practice.

Furthermore, the fact that persons with more than one wife were admitted among the saints in the infant days of the church's history, does not justify such a thing as being warrantable or valid practice today. The primitive churches had many irregularities and disorders which were corrected and in some cases eliminated through the light of the full revelation of Christian doctrine, and by apostolic legislation (Rom. 14:14; 1 Cor. 7:17; 11:16; 14:34,35; Col. 1:25).

As we have seen, then, a man, in order to be a fit subject for admittance into fellowship, must have only one wife. This ruling is further sustained and supported by the apostolic injunction, "Let every man have his own wife, and let every woman have her own husband" (1 Cor. 7:2). It is not unscriptural nor is it an injustice for a man

133

to put away his extra and secondary wives. Indeed it is imperative that a child of God do so. A precedent for such an act is found in the book of Ezra where we have the Jews commanded to put away their heathen wives that they had married besides their Jewish wives—the wives of their youth. (Ezra. 10:3; Mal. 2:14). If this were God's mind then, surely it is no less so today. And if such an act were no hardship to the unregenerate Jews how much more should it not be to a true Christian who is a partaker of divine nature, who has the Holy Spirit unceasingly dwelling in him, and who has a resource of grace in the Lord to enable him to deny ungodliness, and worldly lusts and to live soberly and righteously in this present world (Titus 2:11,12).

REASON FOR DIFFERENCE IN RECEIVING

When chapter ten of this book is compared with chapter nine it will be seen that there is a radical difference in the rules for receiving these two classes; namely, those divorced and remarried after they got converted and those who did so in their unsaved days—*"the pastime of our lives."* The reason for this discrimination in receiving is: that the Christian is under a twofold rule: that of scripture and that of the civil authorities. Whereas the unbeliever, although morally responsible to God His creator, is only under the rule of human government—*"the powers that be"* for his social, moral and political conduct (Gen. 9:1-7; Daniel 2:36-38; Rom. 2:12,14; 13:1-6).

"For where no law is, there is no transgression" (Rom. 4:15) applies in principle to saved and unsaved alike. A Gentile unbeliever is not conscious he is a transgressor when he divorces his mate, if he knows there is no civil law against it. On the other hand a Christian ought to know he is a transgressor when he divorces his wife because the rule of scripture which he is under plainly says such a thing is contrary to the will of the Lord—''and let not the husband put away his wife'' (1 Cor. 7:11).

While one would be careful when admitting a person into fellowship not to lower the scriptural standard of reception and fellowship, yet on the other hand it is needful and obligatory that care be taken not to impose restrictions and make requirements that would go beyond that which is written. For by so doing we may be guilty of defrauding and depriving a believer in Christ of his rightful place and privileges in the Church. Going beyond scripture in the application of it, and the overstatement of a truth has in many instances wrought as much harm as has the perversion of it.

CHAPTER ELEVEN

CONTENTS

Divorce, Remarriage and Church Discipline

Divorce, Remarriage and Church Discipline

We will now take up the subject of discipline as it relates to the *local* Church's corporate responsibility in its care for those in its fellowship. According to the New Testament a local Church is the only corporate body of believers which has divine authority to discipline a Christian. The sphere in which this authority is to be exercised is limited to those of its own number. Notwithstanding these restrictions, the scope of the effects of its disciplinary action extends to all other local churches and should be accepted by them unless discovered to be scripturally unjust. (See Matthew 18:18; 1 Corinthians 1:2; 5:12,13).

Church discipline may be divided into three general classes—*private admonition, public rebuke,* and *excommunication* by the Church. The character of the irregularity determines the mode and measure of the discipline. (See Romans 16:17,18—the *division maker* who is to be marked and avoided; 1 Corinthians 5:13—the *immoralist* who is to be excommunicated; 1 Thessalonians 5:14—the *unruly* who are to be warned, the feebleminded who are to be comforted, and the weak who are to be sustained; 2 Thessalonians 3:14,15—the *willfully disobedient* who are to be admonished as well as having free brotherly intercourse withheld from them; 1 Timothy 5:20—the *public transgressor* who is rebuked before all; Titus 1:10,11—the *vaintalker* who is to have his mouth stopped; 3:10,11—the *heretic* who is to be rejected.)

The lack of one uniform rule among the churches for disciplining divorced persons emanates from the diverse opinions held on the matter. I shall now set forth in detail what I consider to be the order, mode and degree of discipline which would conform to the requirements of Scripture when disciplining divorced persons. A few examples will suffice.

EXAMPLE ONE

QUESTION: WHAT ACTION SHOULD THE CHURCH TAKE TOWARD A BROTHER WHO DIVORCES HIS WIFE ON THE GROUND OF ADULTERY?

ANSWER: Such conduct is contrary to God's mind for the Christian. His will for such is stated in the following words, "Let not the husband put away his wife" (1 Cor. 7:11). It is begging the question to put any qualification whatsoever to this prohibition, as is often done by adding "except for adultery." But the question supposes divorce has taken place. Every case should be judged by its own merits. However, consideration should be given to the fact that the man who divorced his wife may have done it in the conviction that he had scriptural warrant for so doing. Like many more he may have tacitly accepted the unproved assumption that adultery dissolves the marriage union. Moreover, he may have accepted the ruling, which is generally believed among Christians, that the Lord's words of Matthew 5:32 and 19:9, "except it be for fornication," teach it is right for a Christian to divorce on the ground of adultery.

While the act done under such circumstances would not warrant the judgment of expulsion, nevertheless it is serious in its nature and consequences, both to the wife put away and to the local church as God's testimony.* It

---

* By taking the initiative in the divorce action it can be said he freed his wife to enter into a life of marital disorder if she so please.

therefore calls for a milder form of discipline. According to 1 Timothy 3:2,12, blamelessness is a qualification essential to the character of those who rule and serve in the Church. As the person we are considering cannot be said to be blameless in marital relations, it necessarily follows that having taken the initiative in the divorce action he discredited and disqualified himself from doing Christian service, whether it be ruling, pastoring or teaching. The Church is acting within the sphere and scope of its invested and delegated judicial authority (Matt. 18:18; 1 Cor. 5:4,5,12,13), when it prohibits such divorced persons from doing any public functions in its midst.

EXAMPLE TWO

QUESTION: WHAT SHOULD BE THE CHURCH'S ATTITUDE TOWARD A MAN WHO IS THE INNOCENT PARTY IN THE DIVORCE ACTION?

ANSWER: By the term innocent party we mean his conduct was not the cause for the divorce, nor did he take the initiative in instituting divorce proceedings. If no blame is attached to him in the matter, he is not a subject for discipline, and therefore is eligible to serve in the Church in the capacity of his gift and in the measure of his ability. However in every case of divorcement* by Christians, whether it be the innocent party or the guilty one, the "no remarriage rule" applies and must be adhered to as a requisite in being eligible to remain in Church fellowship.

---

* This does not take into consideration cases of annulment in connection with improper marriages.

EXAMPLE THREE

QUESTION: WHAT ACTION SHOULD THE CHURCH TAKE TOWARD A BROTHER WHO DIVORCES HIS WIFE ON ANY GROUND WHATSOEVER OTHER THAN ADULTERY?*

ANSWER: While divorce on the ground of adultery is unscriptural, divorce for any cause less than adultery is a much more serious irregularity when viewed in the light of the fact that in the New Testament there is not one iota of scripture that could possibly be misinterpreted or misused to justify it. Such an act on the part of a Christian is so clearly contrary to God's mind, the character of Christianity, and natural affection that the man who does so stands to have the reality of his Christian profession questioned.

Furthermore, in the light of 1 Timothy 5:8, it is open to question if the Christian who puts away his wife on such grounds may not be guilty of *"not providing for his own,"* and may be classed among those who are said to have denied the faith and become worse than infidels.

The Church should expel from its fellowship any man that is called a brother who divorces his wife for any cause other than adultery. The Christian who is subject to the Word of God and who seeks to honor the name of the Lord Jesus, which is so closely related to the local church, willingly says "amen" to such a ruling.

---

*This does not take into consideration cases of annulment in connection with improper marriages.

EXAMPLE FOUR

QUESTION: WHAT ACTION SHOULD BE TAKEN BY THE CHURCH TOWARD ONE IN ITS FELLOWSHIP WHO AS A DIVORCED PERSON REMARRIES WHILE HIS FORMER PARTNER STILL LIVES?

ANSWER: It is advisable and I would say obligatory, that they who are responsible for the care of God's flock (Acts 20:17,18,28; 1 Thess. 5:12,13; 1 Pet. 5:1-3; Heb. 13:17) visit those who anticipate taking such a step and instruct them in Christ's teaching and that of His apostles on the matter of remarriage by divorced persons. (See Mark 10:11,12; Luke 16:18; 1 Corinthians 7:11,12). These verses are a three-fold witness to the truth that the divorced person who remarries commits adultery by so doing. The penalizing and disruptive consequences resulting from such an act of disobedience should be made clear to them. Many who contemplated such a step often in the conviction that scripture warrants it have been prevented from doing so through such pastoral care having been bestowed upon them. On the other hand for those who receive not the instruction and heed not the warning, but wilfully disobey the Lord's commandment by remarrying, the Church has no other alternative but to act for God's glory, for the honor of the name of the Lord Jesus, and for the maintenance of the holiness feature of God's house. Hence, on the authority of the Word of God which teaches that such a remarriage by a Christian is an adulterous association, the guilty person must be excommunicated from the Church's fellowship (I Cor. 5:12). Alas, what a high price for a Christian to pay for such an act of self-gratification.

141

EXAMPLE FIVE

QUESTION: WHAT ACTION SHOULD THE CHURCH TAKE TOWARD ONE IN ITS FELLOWSHIP WHO IS ELIGIBLE TO MARRY BUT WHO MARRIES A DIVORCED PERSON?*

ANSWER: Scripture teaches that such bear the same degree of guilt as the divorced person whom he or she marries. Both parties are termed adulterers. Therefore, the same measure of discipline, that of excommunication applies to them. This ruling is based on the words of the Lord Jesus, "Whosoever putteth away his wife, and marrieth another committeth adultery; and whosoever marrieth her that is put away from her husband committeth adultery". (Luke 16:18). Such plain scripture needs no comment of mine. It must be perfectly obvious that he who marries a divorced person is alike guilty of adultery.

---

* We have in mind a person who was divorced after becoming a Christian.

CHAPTER TWELVE

CONTENTS

Improper Christian Conduct

Improper Christian Conduct

In the matter of divorce and remarriage there are among Christians two courses of conduct which are diametrically opposite in character and consequence. Many there are who believe they have Scriptural warrant for having divorced their married partners on the ground of adultery. Also among this class are some who believe that they have justification from Scripture for remarrying while their divorced partner still lives. Then there is the class who believe that Scripture does not permit the Christian to divorce. Why these differences? Both classes cannot be scripturally correct. The answer is simple: a Christian's behaviour is the true criterion of how such an one has apprehended the truth.

It will be conceded that on a whole divorces among those who profess to be Christians are based on the words of the Lord Jesus in Matthew 5:32 and 19:9. It will also be admitted that the conviction many Christians have that they should not divorce is also derived from the words of the Lord Jesus in Matthew 19:4-8; Mark 10:6-12; Luke 16:18; I Corinthians 7:10, 11. In other words these two standards of conduct simply conform to the apprehension each have of the words of the Lord.

Generally speaking, Christians who divorce may be able to say. "I am only acting in accordance with Scripture". The scripture is Matthew 5:32 and 19:9. However, I am persuaded by the knowledge of dispensational teaching, the unity of the Scriptures and the perfect use of words by the Lord Jesus when He gave the only cause for divorce, that the Christian is not warranted to use these

145

two Scriptures as ground for divorce. And I am convinced that the one who defends himself in this way is as guilty of the misuse of Scripture and of causing confusion among Christians as he who quotes from the book of Leviticus to justify his not eating certain meats and attempts to enforce his belief upon others.

It may be helpful to cite a few actual incidents to illustrate these two standards of conduct. For the sake of clarity I will group them under two distinct headings —"THE DIVORCE AND REMARRIAGE CLASS" and "THE NO DIVORCE CLASS". The latter to be narrated in chapter thirteen.

THE DIVORCE AND REMARRIAGE CLASS

Speaking from experience we find the majority of people leaning towards the belief that the Christian is warranted by Scripture to divorce and remarry. This numerical superiority seems to have carried weight as evidence and has been one of the factors in influencing people as to which of these two courses of conduct is the scriptural one for the Christian. It will be admitted that the application of such a principle in judging a doctrine or a practice to be right or wrong is unsound and may even be damaging. For example, in the matter of salvation, whether it be obtained by works of righteousness or solely on the principle of faith and as the gift of God it will be readily acknowledged that the greater number teach salvation by works.

Not only are those who believe in divorce more numerous, but their cases are more complex and difficult. We shall look at a few that are quite common and typical.

146

EXPERIENCE ONE

There lived in a small town in the United States of America a married couple whom we shall call Mr. and Mrs. A. Their marriage was an ideal one. They both held things in common and entered together into the enjoyments of life. The time came when a church in the community held revival services which Mrs. A. attended regularly with the result that she professed faith in the Lord Jesus Christ as her own personal Saviour. As would be expected, this wrought a change in her way of living. The grace that had saved her taught her to deny ungodliness and worldly lusts and to live soberly and righteously in this present age (Titus 2:13). Church attendance took the place of the theater, Bible reading displaced former unprofitable reading, the companionship of Christians was desired rather than that of the pleasure loving unconverted. As would be expected, Mr. A. who was an unbeliever, was greatly affected by this change. In course of time he found that his wife's way of living was definitely fixed, which was a surprise, for he had hoped that the effects of her conversion were transitory and would be short-lived.

It soon became evident to Mrs. A. that although her affection for her husband was unchanged and although she continued faithfully to discharge her domestic and conjugal responsibilities towards him, still his love for her was waning. She realized too that he had lost all marital affection for her, which resulted in them being completely estranged from one another, although still living under the same roof. Under such difficult circumstances Mrs. A. continued to live and be governed by the Scripture which says, "And the woman which hath an husband that believeth not, and if he be pleased to dwell with her, let her not leave him'' (I Cor. 7:13). Some time later Mr. A. demanded that she give up her Christian way of living and return to her former habits of life, which were more congenial to him. Because she was unable to comply he deserted her. However, she continued in her Christian course, praying and expectantly hoping for her husband's salvation, knowing this would create a condition that would effect their reconciliation.

But some time afterwards she received a letter through her husband's attorney stating that he desired to be made legally free from her so that the way could be cleared for him to enter into another marriage relation. Her answer to this request was that she was unable to grant it, and that she still hoped for their reconciliation. Nevertheless, under the constant pressure and on the advice of the church leaders she allowed Mr. A. to divorce her. This freed him to remarry, which he did. Now Mrs. A. too feels free to remarry on the mistaken idea that his adultery dissolved their marriage union.

COMMENT

In commenting on this case I would say Mrs. A. is to be commended as well as criticised. She is to be commended for not taking the initiative in separating from her husband, in maintaining the attitude of one ever ready to be reconciled (1 Cor. 7:10), and in not being the party to obtain the divorce. On the other hand she should not have given her husband the unwarranted right to divorce her, for in so doing she shut the door to all hope of being reconciled to him. Furthermore, by illegally freeing him she enabled him to enter a life of marital dis-

order. Her thoughts about herself being made free to remarry are false for they are based (1) on the unproved
assumption that adultery dissolves the marriage bond
and (2) the Lord's teaching in Matthew 5:32 and 19:9
misappropriated.

EXPERIENCE TWO

In narrating the circumstances related to this case I
shall not go into details. It concerns Mr. and Mrs. B. Both
were believers and could number two children born to
them in their marriage union.

Somehow the unexpected happened. Under strong
temptation and in uncommon circumstances Mrs. B. yield-
ed and became unfaithful to her husband by having illicit
relations with some other man. Her husband was one of
the many who held the unproved assumption that adultery dissolves the marriage union. Consequently, upon
learning of his wife's infidelity he considered himself no
longer married to her. Moreover, like many another he
believed that the Lord Jesus in Matthew 5:32 and 19:9,
taught that Christians have the right to divorce their
married partners should such commit adultery against
them. On the strength therefore of these Scriptures he
brought his wife before a court and obtained a divorce.
He also believed that the same Scriptures permitted the
innocent party in the cause of adultery to remarry. As
would be expected he took unto himself another wife.
The second marriage, however, was of short duration,
being terminated by his sudden death.

COMMENT

In considering the facts of this case we can see the
disruptive and harmful consequences which may result

from imperfectly apprehending the truth and by accepting and acting upon an unproved assumption. Mr. B. believed that adultery dissolved the marriage union without having scriptural proof that such a deduction is true.* He also believed that he had the authority of Scripture for his action. But I maintain he was guilty of misinterpreting and misusing the words of the Lord Jesus.

On the other hand Mr. B. either ignored, disobeyed or was ignorant of what Paul the apostle wrote to the Christian. The following apostolic injunction combined with the Lord's own words which are quoted below should have been the deciding factor for Mr. B. as to what was God's will for him. "Let not the husband put away his wife" (I Cor. 7:11), and "Whosoever putteth away his wife, and marrieth another, committeth adultery" (Luke 16:18). Altogether Mr. B.'s conduct manifests on his part, hardness of heart, unnnatural affection, an unforgiving spirit, and willful disobedience to the plain revealed will of God.

EXPERIENCE THREE

The third case that came to my attention some time ago concerns a Mrs. C. who was a Miss K. before her marriage. When a young women, she became a child of God through faith in the Lord Jesus Christ (Gal. 3:26). Her duties in the factory where she was employed brought her into close association with a Mr. C. who made no profession of religion. Mr. C. took an interest in her, which in time developed into a friendship which in turn culminated in an offer of marriage. This presented a serious problem to Miss K. for she was sufficiently acquainted with the Scriptures to know that in marrying Mr. C. she

---

* (See chapter 8 where the scriptural idea of adultery is taught).

150

would be disobeying God by entering into an unequal yoke.

Unfortunately Miss K. at this time was carnal in her mind and backslidden in her ways. When such is the case with a Christian they are ruled by the flesh rather than led by the Holy Spirit and the Word of God. In willful disobedience she consented to marry Mr. C. hoping and consoling herself in the false step she was taking that she would be the means of his conversion—a risky gamble which not a few of the Lord's people have taken to their grief and lifelong sorrow.

After a few years of married life Mrs. C. was restored to the Lord. Naturally her ways of living changed. She confessed to her husband her earlier religious experience of conversion and that she had married him in her backslidden condition. The chance expectation she took in marriage never matured, for Mr. C. remained openly opposed to Christ. Moreover, he considered he had been deceived by his wife for he had not imagined that he was marrying one with such convictions of God, and of the Lord Jesus, and of the Bible. On the ground of this deception he felt justified in deserting her.

One night upon returning from a church service Mrs. C. found a note from her husband stating that he was leaving her and that she should take whatever action she felt appropriate against him. To her credit she waited four years, hoping against hope that her husband might change his mind and be reconciled to her. This hope never materialized. Not having much knowledge of the Scriptures which alone could give her skill to act rightly in the matter, she sought pastoral advice. She was told that owing to lack of proof, she could not divorce her husband on the ground of adultery, but that according to the fifteenth

151

verse of the seventh chapter of first Corinthians she could divorce him for the cause of desertion and be free to remarry. Such advice was surprisingly new to Mrs. C. for she, like many more, tacitly believed the unscriptural assumption that a Christian could divorce for one cause only—namely on the ground of adultery. However, acting on the advice given, Mrs. C. divorced her husband. I understand that up to the time of this writing, although she is not remarried, she would willingly be if the opportunity afforded itself providing such a proposal came from a Christian.

COMMENT

There are a few lessons in the above incident. First, by it the Christian should learn of the danger of not keeping up communion with God (1 John 1:3-7), which is maintained by abiding in Christ, which means, being obedient to His words (John 15:4-10). Secondly we see the personal and practical value of the Christian obeying the words, "Let your light so shine before men, that they may see your good works and glorify your father which is in heaven" (Matt. 5:16). Had these two Christian necessities been maintained daily in the life of Miss K. they would have prevented the unholy friendship from being formed, which led to her unscriptural marriage with all its attendant grief. Thirdly: We see the fulfilment of that unalterable law. "Be not deceived, God is not mocked: for whatsoever a man soweth that shall be also reap" (Galations 6:7). Fourthly: We learn the value and the wisdom of the Scripture which says, "In the multitude of counsellors there is safety" (Proverbs 11:14). Had Mrs. C. sought the advice of not only one man but of a number from among the thousands of gifted and scripturally instructed Bible teachers that are to be found in Christendom she would have been persuaded by their unanimous counsel that she had no grounds whatsoever for divorcing her husband for the cause of desertion.*

---

* The reader is asked to consult chapter 8 of this book where he will find abundant proof given to disprove that 1 Corinthians 7:15; teaches divorce and remarriage on the ground of desertion.

CHAPTER THIRTEEN

CONTENTS

Proper Christian Practice

Proper Christian Practice

We will now consider the class of Christians whose behavior conforms to marriage as constituted by God in the beginning (Gen. 2:24), as taught by the Lord Jesus (Matt. 19:4-8; Mark 10:6-9), and as ordained in all Churches by Paul the apostle (1 Cor. 7:17,39; Eph. 5:31).

THE NO DIVORCE AND NO REMARRIAGE CLASS
CASE ONE

Mr. and Mrs. D. were both Christians. Because of circumstances over which he had no control, Mr. D. was brought into an enforced absence from his wife and family. At the end of this period he returned home to be saddened by the personal confession of his wife that she had been unfaithful to him during their prolonged separation. Naturally he was grieved at what happened. And, as would be expected, he felt bitterly toward her.

The question that confronted him was: What course should he adopt? Should he act according to his feelings, and follow the recognized custom that prevailed among professing Christians, which conformed to the world's low standard. To do this would mean taking his wife before a court and divorcing her on the ground of adultery. On the other hand, he could subordinate his feelings and conform his conduct to Scripture which applies to the Christian. Being a new experience he was at a loss to know how God would have him act.

Fortunately Mr. D. was spiritual, well versed in the Bible, and skilful in the use of Scripture. Fortified with these spiritual qualities he sought the mind of God. In doing this he followed a wise rule by first getting to know all that is written in the Scriptures on divorce. Having ascertained this, the next thing he did was to rightly divide it. He knew that to whom Scripture is spoken is a factor in determining to whom it applies. In applying this rule he found that God had plainly expressed His mind on how a Christian should act in his most distressing circumstances. It was found in the few, simple and unqualified words which Paul wrote, namely "Let not the husband put away his wife" (1 Corinthians 7:11).

I would call the reader's attention to a very significant fact, namely that the Scripture just quoted is the last word spoken by inspiration on divorce. A safe rule to follow (although not generally known) in order to properly appropriate God's mind is to remember that the last words in the progressive revelation of any particular truth supersedes in its application during the dispensation in which it applies, all previous parts of it.

Fortunately, Mr. D. was spiritually minded and as would be expected he obeyed the commandment of the Lord (1 Cor. 7:11) and allowed himself to be motivated by love (Eph. 5:25). He therefore did not put away his erring and repentant partner, but rather forgave her and so obeyed the apostolic injunction that husbands should love their wives even as Christ loved the church and gave Himself for it.

COMMENT

In reviewing this case there are a few valuable and salutary lessons that we may learn and profit from. It teaches the value of being spiritual. One mark of a spiritual man is, that he acknowledges that the things

Paul wrote are the commandmants of the Lord (1 Cor. 14:37). Mr. D. did this very thing in obeying (1 Cor. 7:11). It also shows the profitableness of knowing the Scriptures and of being able to rightly divide them. Had Mr. D. been ignorant of scripture and the knowledge of rightly dividing it he might have misappropriated Matthew 5:32 and 19:9 by applying them to himself when they rightly only apply to Jewish men under the law. And like others he would have simply ignored or explained away the plain words of the Lord to the Christian on the matter of divorce, namely, "Let not the husband put away his wife" (1 Cor. 7:11).

Another thing very evident in this case is: It reveals the weakness of the flesh on the one hand and the power of the spirit and the sufficiency of grace on the other.

It also has in it extenuating circumstances that call for consideration and sympathy. For one thing, the separation was beyond the power of either party. As a rule the prime cause in most of the divorces among professing Christians is connected with marital separation and conjugal rights. This we learn from experience and the following apostolic injunction, "Let the husband render unto the wife due benevolence: and likewise also the wife unto the husband. The wife hath not power of her own body, but the husband: and likewise also the husband hath not power of his own body, but the wife. Defraud ye not another except it be with consent for a time, that ye may give yourselves to fasting and prayer; and come together again, that Satan tempt you not for your incontinency" (1 Cor. 7:3-5).

From the Scripture just quoted we learn that the devil also may be implicated in the immorality that may become the cause in the disruption of a marriage. Were this sufficiently realized by Christians in the married relation they would be more solicitiously minded about being considerate and having due regard for the conjugal rights of one another. It is in the neglecting and withholding of these obligations that Satan is given an opportunity to tempt and ensnare.*

Moreover, it behooves all who are married to be cognizant of the grave dangers that lie in prolonged periods of marital separation. If done it should be by mutual consent, and with due consideration being given to the moral state of the other in view of the self-control that is necessitated by such an undertaking.

CASE TWO

The following incident came to my attention while on a visit to Scotland. It is most exceptional and truly manifests the moral force that Christianity can be for the good of society. To my mind it is a model of the behavior that should characterize the life of the Christian whose marriage has been disrupted on account of adultery or desertion.

It concerns a Mr. E. who in the pastime of his life lived in unrighteousness and ungodliness, but who had a notable conversion to the Lord, to righteousness and to godliness. From the very outset of this change, his wife showed an unsympathetic spirit which later developed to open antagonism toward him and his new way of living. In process of time Mrs. E. evidently tired of being linked with one who was living in the spirit of holiness and in obedience to the Word of God, deserted her husband and went to live with another man. In such circumstances what should Mr. E. do? Two courses of action were open to him: (1) He could follow the precedent of many Christians who

_____
* Where a wife refuses to bear children.

158

believed they were warranted by Scripture to divorce and remarry on the ground of adultery or desertion. (2) He could act on the principle that the marriage union is absolutely indissoluble, and that marriage as originally constituted by God, which does not allow divorce, is the rule to be followed by the Christian. He took the latter course neither divorcing his wife nor giving her the right to divorce him. Furthermore, he acted in accordance with the Scriptural promise, ''How knowest thou, O man, whether thou shalt save thy wife?'' (1 Cor. 7:16), and continued in exercise before God for his wife's salvation keeping the door of his home ever open for her to return and be reconciled. She finally responded to his continual entreaties and was freely and fully forgiven. However, not long after having been shown such grace she once again deserted her husband and returned to her former unlawful association. Did this effect a change in the gracious attitude Mr. E. had shown to his wife and in the course he had adopted— that of not divorcing his wife or allowing her the right to divorce him? It did not.

For many years Mr. E. remained in this trial during which time he glorified God by his walking in love, and through having ''a good report of them which are without'' (1 Tim. 3:7).

After being in this trial for twenty long years Mr. E's wife died under the roof of the man with whom she was living. And here is where the behavior of Mr. E. supremely manifests the love of Christ. Acting on the principle of the indissolubility of the marriage union he recognized his wife as being still joined to him, and believing also that the ''law of the husband'' gave him the right of possession to his wife's body he claimed it and buried her with all the honor to which a wife is entitled.

COMMENT

Christain practice is simply obedience to the letter of Scripture and is after all the true criterion of the way in which one has apprehended the truth and is governed by it. A wrong doctrine can only produce a wrong practice. Of course one may properly apprehend the truth and act in disobedience to it. The fault in such a case would lie in the moral state of the heart.

If there is one thing above others that this experience teaches, it is the value of properly appropriating Scripture and of maintaining a state of heart subjection to the Lord Jesus. These two things were true of Mr. E. Thus he was enabled to triumph on the side of God's will in such distressing circumstances—the rupture of the marriage relation.

REVIEW

The two experiences which I have just related and the three which are narrated in chapter twelve are examples of two standards of conduct which are extremely different in character and in their social effect. While the spiritual and moral state of the Christian may enter into the cause of this difference in behavior on the matter of divorce, still it is quite obvious that the chief factor is the manner in which truth is appropriated. In the main the conduct found in the three experiences related in chapter twelve are the effects of Matthew 5:32 and 19:9 being misinterpreted and misapplied. While on the other hand the high moral standard found in the two experiences narrated in chapter thirteen is the result of the following scriptures: Mark 10:6-12; Luke 16:18; 1 Cor. 7:11, being rightly divided, correctly interpreted and properly applied.

160

Let the reader search the Scriptures from Genesis to Revelation and it will be found that only two classes of persons could legitimately remarry; viz., legally divorced persons under the law (Deut. 24:1-4), and the widow or the widower, be he Jew or Christian.

CHAPTER FOURTEEN

CONTENTS

Too Great a Trial Plea

CHAPTER FOURTEEN

Too Great a Trial Plea

Some may say, "Is not the strict application of the rule 'no divorce and no remarriage'* too high a standard, and if adhered to, will it not work a hardship and be too great a trial to the Christian?" This might be the case with an unbeliever, but surely not for the one who has been made a partaker of divine nature, who is indwelt with the Holy Spirit, who has the love of God shed abroad in his heart, and who has a High Priest which can succor the believer in whatsoever kind of trial he may be found, while doing the will of God.

Furthermore, is not such a plea just reasoning one's way out of the necessity of obedience to the plain command of Christ the Lord (1 Cor. 7:10,11)? It would be as sensible to say that it is too great a hardship for a Christian to remain unmarried and therefore he is justified (when no suitable partner is to be found) in committing fornication or entering into an unequal yoke.

Scripture supposes and God expects that the believer will look upon all his trials in the light of the following Scriptures: "All things work together for good to them that love God" (Rom. 8:28) and "There hath no temptation overtaken you, but such as is common to man: but God is faithful, who will not suffer you to be tempted (tried) above that ye are able, but will with the temptation also made a (the) way of escape that ye may be able to bear it" (1 Cor.. 10:13). We know that God's love is linked with a wisdom that cannot err, and that His way of deliverance is not through disobedience, for God is

---

* Cases of annulment are not considered in this prohibition.

righteous in all His way and always acts in accordance with His written Word.

The substance of apostolic advice to the Christian in such a trial is: He should take it as a trial of his faith (1 Pet. 1:7), and look upon it as suffering as a Christian (1 Pet. 4:16), and for righteousness sake (1 Pet. 3:4). Having done this he should believe in God's love, trust in His power, and continue to wait upon Him to make "the way of escape" which He has promised. And to be always exercised before the Lord for the salvation, or the reconciliation of the erring partner.

THE WAY OF DELIVERANCE

It might be helpful to some who may be passing through the trial of marital disruption if I recount two more experiences which may mirror their case and will show the way in which God graciously brought deliverance.

EXPERIENCE ONE

A Mr. G. who was known for his godliness and spiritual mindedness learned that his wife had secretly committed adultery. He told her of this and gave his forgiveness. In addition to her treacherous act in connection with her marriage covenant Mrs. G. left her husband and became the common-law wife of her accomplice. Had Mr. G. accepted the advice of many of his sympathizers, he would have gone to court and obtained a divorce with the legal right to remarry. However, being a spiritual man he sought obedience to the will of God rather than his own interests. He knew that to put away his wife would be willful disobedience to the command of Christ, "Let not the husband put away his wife" (1 Cor. 7:11). Instead, he preferred to accept his grievous circumstances and difficult situation in the light of what is written in 1 Peter 4:16, "If any man suffer as a Christian let him not be ashamed; but let him glorify God on this behalf."

The chief concern of God in this world is for the good of His people. To this end He will work for their present and eternal good, that He might be glorified in them. For many years Mr. G. remained in this trial, during which time he glorified God by his willing and child-like submission and the maintenance of a godly life. Deliverance came to him quite unexpectantly: his wife was taken away by death in the midst of her unholy alliance.

EXPERIENCE TWO

Mrs. H. was a Christian whose desire was to follow the Lord, which simply means being obedient to the Word of God (1 Sam. 15:11; Matt. 4:4). Her husband made no profession whatever. In course of time he became an alcoholic addict. This naturally was a trial to her, but she took it as from the hand of the Lord while she sought His grace to carry out the injunction, "Likewise ye wives, be in subjection to your own husbands; that if any obey not the word, they also may, without the word, be won by the conversation of the wives" (1 Pet. 3:1,2). Her trial was greatly intensified when he deserted her, leaving her with the full responsibility of rearing their two children.

For several years Mrs. H. knew nothing of his whereabouts, but during all this time she kept the door of their home open for him, so that he might return at his will. According to the law of the State, she could have legally obtained a divorce with the right to remarry. Furthermore, a few Christians advised her that she had scriptural authority for taking such action. They based their claim on 1 Corinthians 7:15 which, they asserted, gave the deserted wife this liberty.*

However, Mrs. H. had other advisors who showed her from Scripture, (which I quote, "And if a woman shall put away her husband and be married to another, she committeth adultery") (Mark 10:12) the immoral consequence of divorce and remarriage. Being spiritually minded, she was enabled by the grace of God and the power of the Spirit to abstain from taking any action whatsoever against her husband.

It is no vain thing, fellow-believer, to commit thy way unto the Lord and with exercise wait upon Him to bring it to pass (Psalms 37:5). This, for which I can vouch, Mrs. H. did. Can you imagine the joy in that household when, after seven years of absence Mr. H. returned, telling her of his conversion (which was most notable) and asking her forgiveness for all the misery he had caused her. As would be expected, she forgave him and restored him to his rightful place: as head, as husband, and as father.

A few years after this, more joy came to this household. Their two children now grown to manhood got saved while attending envangelistic services held in connection with the local church in which Mr. and Mrs. H. were in happy fellowship.

COMMENT

In this case there is much that glorifies God and should encourage the believer who may be in a trial similar to that of Mrs. H. to be obedient to the Word of God. Mrs. H. by obeying the word of the Lord, was preserved from

* See chapter 8 where such a claim is disproved.

166

the path of the destroyer (Psalm 17:4). She was also kept from putting herself in a position by remarriage, where she would have been prevented from giving her husband his rightful place in the home and in the family. And in it we see God fulfilling his words, "For what knowest thou, O wife, whether thou shalt save thy husband?" (1 Cor. 7:16) and "For them that honour me I will honour" (1 Sam. 2:30).

CONCLUSION

CONCLUSION

In the introduction to this treatise, it was stated that one reason I had for writing on the subject of divorce sprang from the conviction that the differences on the matter which are found among Christians were but the consequences of the Lord's words being misappropriated.

I believe this specific misappropriation which is the root cause of these differences has been discovered. It was found to lay in the Christian's misuse of Matthew 5:32 and 19:9.

THE SOLUTION OF THE PROBLEM

The solution of the problem and that which will produce oneness of mind and one uniform rule on divorce and remarriage is found in rightly dividing, correctly interpreting, and properly using the words of the Lord Jesus. I believe I have done this (1) by showing that the term "fornication" used by the Lord does not mean adultery, (2) by pointing out with abundance of proof that Matthew 5:32 and 19:9 are scriptures that belong to the dispensation of the law and apply only to *men* under it who wanted to put away their wives because of finding premarital unchastity in them, (3) by proving that the Christian's use of Matthew 5:32 and 19:9 as his authority to divorce on the ground of adultery is an unwarranted misuse of Scripture, and (4) by proving with irrefutable evidence gained by the use of proved and accredited rules for interpreting the Scriptures, that God's mind for the Christian on the matter of divorce and remarriage is found in the following words: "And unto the married I command, yet not I, but the Lord, Let not the wife depart from her husband: But if she depart, let her remain unmarried, or be reconciled to her husband: and let not the husband put away his wife'' (1 Cor. 7:10,11).

I render heart-felt thanks through our Lord Jesus Christ to our Savior God and Father who by the Holy Spirit exercised and enabled me to produce this written ministry. May He make it profitable for teaching, for reproving, for correcting, for instructing in righteousness to many of His children.

"Now unto Him that is able to keep you from falling, and to present you faultless before the presence of His glory with exceeding joy, to the only wise God our Saviour, be glory, and majesty, dominion and power, both now and ever. Amen'' (Jude 1:24,25).

THE SCRIPTURES EXPLAINED OR CITED